BLAQUE SHOWGIRLS

NAKKIAH LUI

CURRENCY PRESS
The performing arts publisher

GRIFFIN THEATRE COMPANY

CURRENT THEATRE SERIES

First published in 2023
by Currency Press
Gadigal Land, PO Box 2287 Strawberry Hills, NSW, 2012, Australia
enquiries@currency.com.au
www.currency.com.au
in association with Griffin Theatre Company

Copyright: *Blaque Showgirls* © Nakkiah Lui, 2023.

COPYING FOR EDUCATIONAL PURPOSES

The Australian *Copyright Act 1968* [Act] allows a maximum of one chapter or 10% of this book, whichever is the greater, to be copied by any educational institution for its educational purposes provided that that educational institution [or the body that administers it] has given a remuneration notice to Copyright Agency [CA] under the Act.

For details of the CA licence for educational institutions contact CA, 12 / 66 Goulburn Street, Sydney, NSW, 2000; tel: within Australia 1800 066 844 toll free; outside Australia 61 2 9394 7600; fax: 61 2 9394 7601; email: memberservices@copyright.com.au

COPYING FOR OTHER PURPOSES

Except as permitted under the Act, for example a fair dealing for the purposes of study, research, criticism or review, no part of this book may be reproduced, stored in a retrieval system, or transmitted in any form or by any means without prior written permission. All enquiries should be made to the publisher at the address above.

Any performance or public reading of *Blaque Showgirls* is forbidden unless a licence has been received from the author or the author's agent. The purchase of this book in no way gives the purchaser the right to perform the play in public, whether by means of a staged production or a reading. All applications for public performance should be addressed to the author c / - Left Bank Literary, email grace@leftbankliterary.com.

Typeset by Brighton Gray for Currency Press.

Front cover shows Stephanie Somerville, photo by Brett Boardman, design by Alphabet.

Currency Press acknowledges the Traditional Owners of the Country on which we live and work. We pay our respects to all Aboriginal and Torres Strait Islander Elders, past and present.

 A catalogue record for this book is available from the National Library of Australia

Contents

BLAQUE SHOWGIRLS   1

Theatre Program at the end of the playtext

Blaque Showgirls was first produced by Malthouse Theatre and Triple R at the Merlyn Theatre, Kulin Nation, Melbourne, on 11 November 2016 with the following cast:

MOLLY	Emi Canavan
CHANDON	Elaine Crombie
GINNY JONES	Bessie Holland
KYLE McLACHLAN / TRUE LOVE INTEREST	Guy Simon

Director, Sarah Giles
Dramaturg, Declan Greene
Contributing Dramaturg, Louise Gough
Set and Costume Designer, Eugyeene Teh
Lighting Designer, Paul Jackson
Composition and Sound Designer, Jed Palmer
Movement Direction, Ben Graetz

CHARACTERS

GINNY/SARAH JANE JONES
CHANDON
AUNTY MAVIS
NARRATOR
AUDIENCE MEMBER 3
KYLE McLACHLAN
THE BOARD
AUDIENCE MEMBER 1
MOLLY, Irish accent.
MERCH BOY
CLARINDA
KANGAROO METER MAID
HOST
AUDIENCE MEMBER 2
TRUE LOVE INTEREST
STAGE HAND
HECKLER, Irish.
LEAVES
SUPER SCROLL

NOTES

A slash (/) in a character's line denotes where the following character's line should begin.

A slash (/) at the beginning of a line denotes a complete overlap with the following character's line. A (…) at the end of a line indicates a trail off. A (…) indicates a pause/silence. A (—) indicates a sudden stop.

This play exists in alternative world where everything is based on shallow stereotypes and sex and culture are big commodities. A melodrama in the style of *Showgirls* meets *South Park*.

CONTENT WARNING

(Largely satirical) depictions of blood and gore, drug use, murder, racism, sexism, sexual abuse, physical violence, weapons, and partial nudity. The play also contains references to death and dying, homophobia and genitalia.

This play text went to press before the end of rehearsals and may differ from the play as performed.

SCENE 1: STAGE

NARRATOR: [*voiceover*] In the dreamtime ...

Didgeridoo ... clapsticks ...

... when stories, myth and culture were born from sacred life ...
When terra nullius became terra fullius ...

A mob of Blaquefullas decided put the sensation back in self-determination! They want you to recognise between their thighs. Go on a journey with them to the realms of desire, let their cultural empowerment light you on fire!

Ladies and gentlemen, boys and girls—please leave: anyone under eighteen is legally prohibited from this venue.

Awkward beat as people leave.

Please welcome to stage ... doing her signature dance ...

Music ramps up ... CHANDON's husky voice fills the room as the lights and sound do something cool.

CHANDON: [*voiceover*] There was a dance passed down to me ... a dance that has survived over sixty-five thousand years ... The dance of my people ... of the irresistible, the inviting, the most impassioned Indigenous bird of this land ...

NARRATOR: [*voiceover*] Presenting ... Chandon Connors in the Cheeky Bin Chook Dance!

CHANDON appears fully in the spotlight, lit up in all her glory as a Sexy Ibis.

CHANDON: It's Bin Chicken ... or as I call it ...

[*Pronouncing like 'bin chicken'*] Been Cheeky ... Time!

CHANDON does an extravagant dance number to a sexy, fast-paced song with an 'Aboriginal' tone.

She finishes the dance looking nude and amazing. The play title is shown:

'BLAQUE SHOWGIRLS'.

SCENE 2: CHITOLE COMMUNITY HALL

Backstage. Chitole (pronounced like fancy 'shithole') Community Hall. Run-down local hall of a small country town. Decades old lino dresses the floor. Scrappy, dirty streamers hang up across the sides of the walls.

HOST: That was Jennifer and the Jenniferettes! Thanks Jen!
Introducing the next contestant in the 'Chitole Community Talent Contest' … It's Sarah Jane Jones. Again.

> GINNY *(Sarah Jane), 18–20s, walks on stage, painted up in an Aboriginal-esque costume with glitter and leaves but it's all a bit shit.*

GINNY: Hello, my name is Sarah Jane Jones. I am a young, proud Aboriginal woman. And I'm going to perform the Cheeky Bin Chook. The signature dance of my idol, Chandon Connors. Again.

> GINNY *gets into position. Tacky 'Aboriginal' music starts to play.* GINNY *rises to start her dance until she starts to get heckled by the very ocker, rural sounding audience. (They can also be offstage. Up to you.)*

AUDIENCE MEMBER 1: Get off!
AUDIENCE MEMBER 2: You suck!
AUDIENCE MEMBER 1: You're not even bloody Aboriginal!
AUDIENCE MEMBER 3: Dirty bird!
AUDIENCE MEMBER 2: Dickhead!
AUDIENCE MEMBER 3: Inside-out coconut!
AUDIENCE MEMBER 1: This is cultural appropriation!
GINNY: No it's not! I'm Aboriginal!
AUDIENCE MEMBER 3: Yeah but Chandon Connors isn't from here! She's from somewhere else!
GINNY: So? I'm Aboriginal!
AUDIENCE MEMBER 1: The First Nations community is made of many different and varied groups from all over the country who have their own unique cultural practices and traditions, ya dumb cunt!
GINNY: Yeah … well … you're just scared of a beautiful strong Black woman!

AUDIENCE MEMBER 3: You're not Black!
GINNY: Yes I am!
AUDIENCE MEMBER 2: Yeah, sure you are! You're white chocolate!
AUDIENCE: White Chocolate! White Chocolate! White Chocolate! White Chocolate!
GINNY: Shut up! Shut up! Shut up! Just shut up!
You're nothing but a bunch of redneck crackers! I hate you! I hate everyone in Chitole! I hate you all!

GINNY *runs offstage in tears.*

SCENE 3: BY THE RIVER

A group of Aboriginal people sit by the river. They see GINNY *approach and roll their eyes; the crazy white girl is back again.* AUNTY MAVIS *(older Aboriginal woman) is upset at her arrival.*

AUNTY MAVIS: Oh no, not her again.
GINNY: Aunty! Aunty! Aunty!
AUNTY MAVIS: Look, I've told you this before, I'm not your / Aunty.
GINNY: / Oh Aunty! Aunty! I just did the talent contest and it was so awful. All I wanted was to share some of our culture with them. But they were so racist to me. Calling me names! Oh, they called me so many names.
Like 'Inside-Out Coconut', 'White Chocolate', 'Dickhead'.
Do you even know what it's like to be judged by the colour of your skin?!
AUNTY MAVIS: I might have an idea.
GINNY: If only I was dark like you. Then things would be easier.
AUNTY MAVIS: Listen, Sarah Jane, have you ever considered that maybe … well, maybe you're not … not from this side of town. Get what I'm saying? Not from this side of town.
GINNY: But of course I am, Aunty Mavis!
I remember it like it was yesterday.
Me, a baby in my cot … and there's Mum, looking down at me … Her beautiful Black skin glistening as she smiles.
It's why I'm so good at dancing.
It's why I feel a connection to you mob!

AUNTY MAVIS: Well, connection would be pushing it. I really wouldn't say we have a / connection.
GINNY: / It's why I feel at home by the river, why I have a connection with the land … why I love dirt.

    GINNY *picks up some dirt and rubs it against her face.*

[*Whispering*] I love you, dirt.
AUNTY MAVIS: Yes, yes, the dirt's real nice.

    AUNTY MAVIS *slaps the dirt out of her hands.*

GINNY: Hey!
AUNTY MAVIS: Look, Sarah Jane, you're a … nice … little … gin. A real nice *gin*. But this has gone on long enough. It's about time you knew about your mother.
GINNY: What do you know about my mum?

    AUNTY MAVIS *pulls out a box that says 'SECRET STUFF'.*

AUNTY MAVIS: It's a bit of Chitole town secret and we don't like to talk about it … but your mother was …
Well … see for yourself.

    AUNTY MAVIS *shoves* GINNY *the photo.* GINNY's *eyes slowly light up in realisation.*

GINNY: It's my mother! And she IS Black!
AUNTY MAVIS: Well, in a / way …
GINNY: / Wait—is that the Blaque Showgirls sign?
AUNTY MAVIS: Listen / Sarah Jane—
GINNY: / Oh my god! My mum was a Blaque showgirl?! An actual Blaque Showgirl!
AUNTY MAVIS: Sarah Jane, listen to / me—
GINNY: / It all makes sense! It's a sign! I never felt like I belonged here. Except with the dirt.

    GINNY *lovingly strokes the dirt.*

AUNTY MAVIS: Stop that! It's weird. Sarah Jane, I know you're thick and all but—
GINNY: / I'm leaving Chitole! Right this very moment! And I'm never coming back!
AUNTY MAVIS: No, Sarah Jane—Wait—what? You're leaving? Finally?

GINNY: Yes!
Right now!
Why, Aunty? Do you have something to tell me?
AUNTY MAVIS: Ahhh ... no. Nothing at all. Wouldn't want to keep you!
GINNY picks up a handful of dirt. She rubs it softly against her face.
GINNY: Don't worry sweet dirt, I'd never leave you.
GINNY throws a bunch of dirt into her backpack.
Goodbye Chithole, goodbye Sarah Jane Jones. Blaque Showgirls, here I come!
GINNY waves good bye and runs away from the river, from Chitole, bound for BrisVegas.
AUNTY MAVIS: Thank fuck she's gone.

SCENE 4: BRISVEGAS

Montage of GINNY travelling to BrisVegas.

GINNY runs down the side of the empty country highway. She holds her suitcase close to her chest.

She stands by the side of an isolated long stretch of highway in the Australian red desert. She holds out her thumb in a tantalising manner, almost as if she'll seduce a car out of thin air.

GINNY arrive in darkness. BrisVegas unfolds around her: it's bright and bold and brassy.

People spruik her flyers. It's like Mt Druitt Food Court meets the Gold Coast meets Las Vegas postcard.

A KANGAROO METER MAID hops past GINNY. She waves at it merrily. The KANGAROO eyes GINNY over and hops over to her.

KANGAROO: Hi Ginny!
GINNY: Who are you?
KANGAROO: I'm a meter maid! Here's a fine ... for being so fine! Welcome to BrisVegas!
GINNY: Wow! It's so glamorous here!
KANGAROO: Let me show you around! Anything you want—BrisVegas has it! There is Corroboree Club, Uluru Rock Cafe, Ethnic Emporium,

Girls Gone Native, Dirty Dumplings, WetWetWaterholes, Red Rooters, ShameJobHandJobs, YouSpearEmWeGrillEm!

> *Some guy opens up his jacket and on the inside there are rows of gold boomerangs.* GINNY *inspects them.*

Now!

> *Suddenly the* KANGAROO *grabs her suitcase, a fight ensues between* GINNY *and the* KANGAROO *over the suitcase.*

Hahaha! Takers keepers!

GINNY: Give it back! Give it back!

KANGAROO: This is BrisVegas, slut!

> GINNY *loses her grip and the* KANGAROO *hops away with her suitcase, laughing evilly.*

GINNY: Come back you thieving kangaroo! Oh, my dirt! My special, special dirt! Where will I ever get more dirt?!

> GINNY *falls to the ground and rolls in dirt and cries. A big paper ad for Blaque Showgirls get swept down the stage, straight into* GINNY*'s face. She swats it away.*

My dirt!

> GINNY *laments and the paper comes flying back into* GINNY*'s face. She swats it away.*

What am I going to do?

> *The paper comes back this time and refuses to leave, covering* GINNY*'s face as she attempts to get rid of it.*

Go the frick away you fricking piece of paper! Wait—wait there.

> GINNY *unfolds the paper.*

'Auditions for Blaque Showgirls' newest show! "Dreamtime Extravaganza: Rider of the Rainbow Serpent!" Are your nipples brown enough for the world's best cultural carnival?'

> GINNY *looks down her shirt at her nipples.*

No … but they can be.

This is fate! You can take away my dirt! You can take away my bag! But you can't take away my dreams or this piece of paper!

KANGAROO *hops back and steals her piece of paper.*

Hey!

KANGAROO: Hahaha gotcha again! Slut!

SCENE 5: CROWN CASINO GOLD / SHOWROOM

GINNY *stands with a group of auditionees in the decadent foyer of the Crown Casino Gold. Her clothes are all tattered and she is covered in dirt, looking out of place amongst the glamour.* GINNY *takes it all in, full of wonder.*

KYLE McLACHLAN, *38, ponytail-hair-having, suit-wearing, enters and stands in front of over a hundred auditionees. He is open-shirted with a string of red, black and yellow Aboriginal beads around his neck and an expensive watch on his wrist. This is one smooth operator. He also always checks his phone a lot. Probs on coke. He's THAT guy.*

KYLE: Listen up, bitches!

You're at the auditions of 'Blaque Showgirls'.

The biggest, bestest Aboriginal-led and performed culturally and sexually authentic dance revue in all of BrisVegas! Some say ALL OF WORLD!

Cheers.

So you better listen hard and listen good.

My name is Kyle McLachlan and I'm a proud First Nations man from the Smugcunce nation. I run this joint.

SCROLL SUPER: NOT THE REAL KYLE McLACHLAN.*

*FOR LEGAL REASONS WE HAVE TO SHOW THIS SO YOU REALISE THIS IS NOT AN ACTUAL REPRESENTATION OF THE ACTOR 'KYLE McLACHLAN'.

KYLE: Before we go any further, I'd like to acknowledge the owners of this building … Steggles Chicken. 'Steggles: the other white meat!'

Applause.

You're all here today because of our bran new show: 'Dreamtime Extravaganza: Rider of the Rainbow Serpent'!

Today is a once-in-a-lifetime opportunity.

The pressure's on.

We want freshness
We want newness.
And definitely NO uglies.
I can already tell there are some smudge muffins in the crowd. Any questions?

GINNY: Where's Chandon?

'Yeahs' echo her throughout the crowd.

KYLE: Chandon doesn't come to the general auditions. This isn't a meet-and-greet where you pay a hundred dollars to get a picture on your iPhone and tell your squashed omelette friends that you got to meet Chandon Connors like a bunch of fucking losers. THIS IS AN AUDITION FOR THE BLAQUE SHOWGIRLS!

GINNY: Soo … Chandon isn't coming?

KYLE: No. No she's not.

GINNY: When do we get to meet her?

'Yeahs' echo her throughout the crowd. Again. Agitating KYLE.

KYLE: Shut up! You only get to meet her if you're accepted into the show. Now—shirts off. Nipple examination time!

SMOKE BOMB! CHANDON CONNORS, *ageless, the very epitome of Glamour. She wears a jumpsuit with a bedazzled Aboriginal design.* GINNY *is in awe that her idol is standing there right in front of her.*

CHANDON *and* KYLE *have some serious sex vibes going on, a constant game of 'Are They Or Aren't They?'*

Jesus Christ! Chandon! Where did you come from?!

CHANDON: None of your business. You're having auditions without me, Kyle?

KYLE: Just a few general auditions. Nothing major, Chandon.

CHANDON: I pick my ensemble. Me.

CHANDON *walks up and down inspecting the auditionees.*

Same old, same old. A few smudge muffins I see.

Notices GINNY.

What's that?

KYLE: That? I suppose that's our first auditionee.

CHANDON *circles* GINNY, *inspecting her ... sniffing her ... Sexily.*
CHANDON: But it's ... very ... white.
KYLE: [*reading from paperwork*] Apparently she's Black. On the mother's side.
CHANDON: Where are you from? Who's your mob?
KYLE: We're on a strict schedule, Chandon.
[*To* GINNY] Nipples out please.
GINNY *goes to take off her shirt but hesitates.*
CHANDON: Hurry up!
GINNY *quickly takes her shirt off.* KYLE *inspects her nipples.*
KYLE *ticks and makes scribbles on the forms.*
KYLE: Hmmm. Yes. Fine areola size. Unusually long nipple length.
CHANDON: And pink. Her nipples are pink, Kyle. You. What's your name?
GINNY *is speechless.*
I'm talking to you, Pink Nips! Who. Are. You?
GINNY: My name is ... is ...
CHANDON: Is what?
GINNY: My name is ... is ...
AUNTY MAVIS: [*voiceover*] You're a nice little gin ... a real nice gin like you ... A nice little gin like you—
GINNY: Gin!
CHANDON: Gin?
GINNY: Ginny! I'm Ginny!
CHANDON: Your name is Ginny?
GINNY: Yes. It's short for Ginnifer.
CHANDON: Your name is Ginnifer?
GINNY: Yes but people call me Ginny. My fellow blakfullas. My mob. They call me Ginny. Ginny Jones. That's my name. And I'm your biggest fan, Miss Connors.
CHANDON: Of course you are.
GINNY *reaches out to try and touch* CHANDON *but* CHANDON *slaps her hand away.*
No touching!

KYLE: What dance have you prepared for us today?
GINNY: I have a bunch of dances I could do for you.
   There is the Little Emu, the Gatherer Emu, the Sorry Emu, the Tastes Like Chicken Emu, the WhatHappenedtotheIceBucketChallenge Emu and, of course, the Cheeky Bin Chook.
CHANDON: HA!
   You do realise the Cheeky Bin Chook is one of the hardest bird dances there is.
GINNY: Yes, Miss Connors. I've watched you do it a million times.
CHANDON: It takes more than a few bird dances to be a Blaque Showgirl. NEXT!
GINNY: Maybe you should see them first!
CHANDON: Look—the pink pussy scratches. Well gorn then, darlin'. Do the Cheeky Bin Chook then. DANCE!

> *Everything goes quiet. The entire focus is on* GINNY. *She gets in her starting position. Just as she begins to dance, she starts to hear the sounds of her past.*

AUDIENCE: [*voiceover*] White Chocolate! White Chocolate! White Chocolate!
GINNY: SHUT UP! SHUTUP! SHUTUP!

> GINNY *falls to the ground crying, mortified, as everyone laughs.*

CHANDON: I don't know what you just did but that is definitely no Bin Chook. Next!

> GINNY *runs off in tears. Just like that, her dream is gone.*

SCENE 6: BRISVEGAS / STREET

GINNY *sits on a step with a dirty blanket around her shoulders holding a foam cup.* MOLLY, *a young (18–20s) Aboriginal woman wearing pale white make-up with freckles and a red wig, rides past on an eBike covered with green shit. She speaks in an inconsistent, terrible Irish accent.*

MOLLY *spots* GINNY *and then reverses back.* MOLLY *looks at* GINNY *sympathetically and throws a bunch of coins in her cup.*

GINNY: Hey! Be careful! I was drinking that!

MOLLY: I am so sorry! I thought you were begging for money.
GINNY: Why?! Because I'm Black?!
MOLLY: No, because you were holding out a foam cup and have a dirty blanket around your shoulders.
GINNY: What blanket?

Notices the blanket.

It's not a blanket! Get it off me! Get it off me!

The BLANKET THING *stands up and runs away. Chaos! Screams! From* GINNY*! From* MOLLY*! From the* BLANKET THING*!*

MOLLY: Shoo, Blanket Thing! Shoo! I'm Molly.
GINNY: I'm Ginny.
MOLLY: What brings you to BrisVegas, Ginny?
GINNY: I'm meant to be following my dream. To be a Blaque Showgirl. Just like my mum … Before she … before she died.
MOLLY: I'm so sorry, Ginny.
GINNY: It's okay. She died a long time ago. In a freak smoking ceremony when I was only three years old.
MOLLY: Really?
GINNY: The doctors said that the amount of eucalyptus smoke I consumed in the accident should have given me brain damage, but it didn't affagatoo me at all.
MOLLY: You mean affect?
GINNY: That's it. It doesn't affagatoo me at all.
MOLLY: You just said / afoo—
GINNY: / That's one of the reasons I'm here.
MOLLY: To see a neurological specialist?
GINNY: To follow in my mum's footsteps. But look at me. All my stuff stolen and nowhere to live. Just like my Aboriginal ancestors.
MOLLY: You're so lucky! I never knew my ancestors.
GINNY: The Irish?
MOLLY: You think I'm Irish?!
GINNY: Yeah, why?
MOLLY: Well, nobody ever thinks I'm Irish.
GINNY: They don't? Why not?
MOLLY: Well, because … and this might come as a shock … I used to be Aboriginal.

GINNY: What?!

> MOLLY *takes off some her make up and holds her wig up: there is dark skin and dark hair.* GINNY *holds up her fingers in the sign of the cross.*

Hey! Looky here shapeshifter! I don't need no trouble!

MOLLY: No, no! It's just make-up and a wig! See … I grew up Aboriginal but I always felt this connection to white culture, ya know? I loved Simply Red, John Farnham, wearing a sweater around my shoulders and I've always had this, like, inherent supremacy where I just knew I was better, ya know?

Anyways, last year, on a Contiki tour through the UK, I stood on a bog in Dublin … and it was like I could feel the land underneath me and I just knew I was from there.

So I came home and did a 23andMe test and it turns out my great-great-great grandfather was Irish! Yeah! Wild right?!

GINNY: Wow!

MOLLY: Which explains my love of potatoes and clogs and windmills—

GINNY: Aren't clogs and windmills Dutch?

MOLLY: I think I know what's Irish, Ginny. It's in my blood. But most of all it explains my passion and gift for River Dancing. Wanna see?

GINNY: Spose so.

> MOLLY *plays some Irish music and* MOLLY *starts River Dancing. She's terrible but the look on her face is filled with pride. Suddenly she gets hit with a potato and an* IRISH HECKLER *yells!*

HECKLER: [*voiceover*] Stop that, ya Connor Come Lately! It's offensive!

> MOLLY *picks up the potato, smiling and waving.*

MOLLY: Thank you for the potato!

[*To* GINNY] Us Irish are always looking out for each other after the potato famine.

Cheer up! If you need money, you can come work with me at the Irish pub.

You have to work topless or as they refer to it, nipple affirmative.

It's really classy like that. Really classy. Like really, really classy.

GINNY: What's it called?

MOLLY: The Cream of Cunty Mayo.
It's an Irish-slash-mashed-potato-slash-topless-River-Dancing bar. I work there at night and do food delivery during the day.
Topless River Dancing is a very, very dangerous art form. Especially hazardous to eyes. So they are always looking for new girls with fresh eyeballs.
GINNY: I have eyeballs!
MOLLY: Come on then! I'm late for my shift!
GINNY: But how will they think I'm white when I'm Black!
MOLLY: We'll lie. Just a wee lie.
GINNY: ... So what you're saying is ... It's IRISH MAKEOVER TIME!

> MOLLY *conjures Irish magic into air. Irish music! Stars! Explosions! Lights! A* LEPRECHAUN *comes out and starts circling* GINNY. *All of sudden she is transformed into a sexy leprechaun and* MOLLY *a sexy River Dancer.*

SCENE 7: CREAM OF CUNTY MAYO

The Cream of Cunty Mayo. Irish paraphernalia hangs outside and a big flashing fluorescent sign that has a leprechaun being Bukkake'd in lights around them.

MOLLY: Here we are! The Cream of Cunty Mayo!
GINNY: Whoa! How did you do that?
MOLLY: Do what?
GINNY: Magically transform me and teleport us here. Where did the leprechaun go?
MOLLY: Ginny, we walked into the back room and my manager, Seamus, put that on you.
GINNY: No! A magic LITTLE GREEN LEPRECHAUN DANCED AROUND ME, JUGGLING POTATOES ON A RAINBOW OF GOLD! NOT ONE OF THOSE GAY RAINBOWS! And turned me into this!
MOLLY: Sure, Ginny, sure. Working at the Cunty Mayo is easy. All you have to do serve mashed potato, Guinness and River Dance sexily on stage. If anyone asks you to do anything, just say 'Diddly-dee, no speak Inglish, only Gaelic!'

GINNY: 'Diddly-dee, no speak Inglish, only Gaelic!'
MOLLY: Perfect! Let's start!

> KYLE *and* CHANDON *enter, full of power and sex, but don't see* MOLLY *and* GINNY *yet.*

GINNY: No, Molly, I can't. It's the people from Blaque Showgirls!
MOLLY: Kyle and Chandon?
GINNY: Yes! I have to hide!
MOLLY: Ginny, wait! Come back!

> GINNY *does a little jump and taps her heels in the air then runs off like leprechaun as* MOLLY *chases her.*

> KYLE *and* CHANDON *take a seat. Their sex vibe is strong.*

KYLE: Why did you insist on coming to this cum den, Chandon?
CHANDON: Don't be such a snob, Kyle. I like it here. It's charming. The Irish are our comrades against the colonisers, one could say. And besides, when have you ever been afraid of a little cum? Or a little … colon-sensation?
KYLE: [*grunting in pleasure*] Funny Chandon, very funny but this is a new suit and this seat is sticky.

> CHANDON *runs her finger into the grime of the seat and holds it up to* KYLE*'s mouth expectantly.*

CHANDON: Loosen up, Kyle, have a little fun. Taste the cream of cunty mayo.

> CHANDON *pushes her finger into* KYLE*'s mouth and he rejoices it, grunting.*

Kyle, have you ever thought of being your own boss?
KYLE: Like LuLaRoe or Herbalife? Working from home and getting people to sell on your downline and you take a percentage of their profits?
CHANDON: No, that's a pyramid scheme. I'm talking about Blaque Showgirls.
KYLE: Chandon, you're the lead and I'm the CEO. We are the bosses. Duh.
CHANDON: I'm talking about the board.
KYLE: Aren't the board great! A good group of men. Real men. Businessmen.

CHANDON: White men.
> *For some reason* KYLE *gives a grunt of pleasure.*

KYLE: Yes. Real white businessmen.

CHANDON: The board are getting restless, Kyle. Haven't you noticed? Insisting on a whole new show—

KYLE: / They don't think there's been enough audience growth.

CHANDON: It's not us that needs to change! This show could be an opportunity to do something new.
Something that appeals to a whole new audience. Not just the same old shit with a new ribbon.

KYLE: We're all ribbon, not shit, Chandon and you can't tie shit in ribbon because it's all squishy and yuck. What are you getting at?

CHANDON: Right now one hundred percent of our audiences are white.

KYLE: Are you including the little family of rats that live under the stage?

CHANDON: Okay, ninety-nine-point-nine percent of the audience are white, but we could be building a new audiences, a new community: other Blaque women, Blaquefullas, Women of Colour—

KYLE: / The little garden gnomes that come to life when you look away!
> KYLE *looks around.*

Wait, is that why you brought me here—
> CHANDON *grabs* KYLE*'s face. Sexily.*

CHANDON: Focus, Kyle. Maybe it's time to give the people something different.
These white men have been in charge for too long. Myself and some of the other Blaque Showgirls have been buying shares since the company started. We now own forty-nine percent of the company.
> KYLE *gets turned on.*

KYLE: Why do you need me?

CHANDON: I need you to sign me over your shares and then I will be the majority shareholder.

KYLE: What's in it for me?

CHANDON: We dissolve the board and fill the board with First Nations women. We appoint you as Chair, I become CEO, and we run Blaque Showgirls.

KYLE: [*turned on*] Chandon … are you talking about a hostile takeover?

CHANDON: It's not hostile if we are taking over what has always been ours. Blaque showgirls by Blaque Showgirls owned by Blaque Showgirls. For us. By us. Entirely.

KYLE: Chandon … it's hard.

CHANDON: You're always hard.

KYLE: No, the plan.

CHANDON: All you have to do is sign.

KYLE: Chandon … I never told you this but remember that sex party in the penthouse pool with the board a couple of years ago.

CHANDON: Which one?

KYLE: The one with the sniff-and-scratch stickers.

CHANDON: Vaguely.

KYLE: Well, in the midst of passion … they asked me to make a blood oath with them … They would let me be CEO forever if I never FUCK UP! … but if I did … then they chop off my dick.

CHANDON: Why the fuck would you agree to that?

KYLE: It was in the midst of passion, Chandon! We all made it! The board and me!

CHANDON: Kyle, I'm tired of doing all the work but not owning a piece of the pie. I'm going to have majority shares one way or another. If you're not with me, you're against me and we all know how that turns out.

KYLE: Okay, I propose this: you make sure this new show is our best show yet and I'll sign you my shares. Deal.

CHANDON: Deal.

The shake but CHANDON *doesn't let go of* KYLE*'s hand.*

I know you like being a bottom but if you fuck me on this, Kyle, you'll be bottomed by my heel so far up your ass that it will push you down to hell and then past hell until you're on top of the world singing 'Glory to the New Blaque Queen'.

CHANDON *pulls out a razored boomerang on* KYLE *out of nowhere.*

And then I'll boomerang both of your balls off.

KYLE: Nice try, Chandon. But I don't have any balls.
Let's toast!

KYLE *clicks his fingers in the air (like an asshole) to get the attention of* MOLLY *and* GINNY.

Whose ass do I have to eat to get a drink around here?

KYLE *sees* MOLLY *dragging* GINNY *in with her. He snaps his fingers again like a twat.*

Hey! I've been waiting!

MOLLY: Diddly dee! How I can help you?

CHANDON: Wait ... is that you? Alinta? Kyle, it's Alinta!

MOLLY: My name is Molly now. I told you.

KYLE: What's on your face? Why do you look like that?

CHANDON *suddenly notices* GINNY.

CHANDON: Oh look, if it isn't little Ginny Jones. The whitest little Black girl who does the best emu dances around.

GINNY: Diddly-dee, no speak Inglish, only Irish!

MOLLY: Gaelic!

GINNY: No, I'm straight!

CHANDON: You really are one confused little gin, aren't you Ginny? First you're Black and now you're white.

GINNY: I'm not white!

CHANDON: Maybe you're better at being white than you are Black? Shall we see, little Ginny Jones? Shall we see?

What dances do you do here?

MOLLY: We do all the dances: Angela's Asses, CuntyClovers, the Gushing Guiness, the TIT of the IRA, Get Down with the Car Bomb Diggity (no really, get down and cover your heads), the Girth of Colin Firth and of course, the Liam Neeson Strip Revue named after Ireland's most attractive and violent man.

CHANDON *slams money down.*

CHANDON: One Angela's Asses please!

Angry Dance Sequence:

The lights go crazy and some Irish song ('I'm Shipping Up to Boston' by Dropkick Murphys). MOLLY *starts to perform a sexy River Dance.* GINNY *follows* MOLLY*'s lead.*

As they dance, CHANDON *and* KYLE *watch with mocking laughter.*

> GINNY *catches sight of herself in the mirror.*
>
> *She can't take it anymore!*
>
> GINNY *breaks out of the Angela's Asses dance and starts dancing with wild abandon. She tears off her leprechaun uniform.*
>
> *The music and the lights change.*
>
> GINNY*'s wild dancing turns into an energetic, traditional-meets-modern dance routine.*
>
> *She finishes and everyone in Cunty Mayo cheers.*
>
> GINNY *goes to run away but* KYLE *appears and stops her.*

KYLE: Look, Ginny, I liked your dancing. I liked it a lot. There's something unique about you.
    You're so wild. So raw. So … so … I can't quite put my finger in it … I mean … on it. I mean …

GINNY: You mean what?

KYLE: Well, it's a shame about your nipple colour. Maybe you could've had a future at Blaque Showgirls.

> GINNY *does a dramatic cry and goes to run away but runs straight into* CHANDON, *who has appeared (or just walked over) in front of her.*

CHANDON: You run away too much, Ginny Jones. One day you'll have to stop running and face whatever you're running from.

GINNY: Stop toying with me okay! I have nothing! I am nothing! Just like my dead mother!

> CHANDON *sshhhh's* GINNY *then runs a finger down* GINNY*'s face and lifts up her chin. Sexily.*

CHANDON: Ssshhhh.
    Poor lost little thing. Stand still.

> CHANDON *circles* GINNY, *sexily, inspecting her, sexily.*

    She can have a trial.

GINNY: What?

KYLE: What are you doing, Chandon?

CHANDON: We're changing up the show right? Doing something different? Let's do it. I might be a cunt but I'm fair. Maybe little

Ginny Jones isn't completely deprived of talent. Maybe she takes after her mother after all.

CHANDON smoke-bombs it out of there.

KYLE: What do you say, pussycat?
GINNY: Yes! Yes! Of course, Mr McLachlan!
KYLE: Just bring in your Confirmation and I'll see you in rehearsals.
GINNY: Confirmation?
KYLE: Your Confirmation of Aboriginality. You've got one, right? A certificate to prove that you're recognised and accepted as an Aboriginal person by your community. You have that right?
GINNY: Of course. Totally. Totally accepted. Totally have one. Ol' accepterooney over here. Accepted lots and lots. In fact, they that accept me too much. If you know what I mean?
KYLE: Do you mean sexually?
GINNY: Do I?
KYLE: I'm asking you.
GINNY: And I'm asking you.

They stare off.

KYLE: Okay. Great.
See you at rehearsals, doll. Don't forget the certificate.

KYLE leaves. MOLLY runs over to GINNY to congratulate her.

GINNY: Molly! Chandon wants me in Blaque Showgirls—but they want a Confirmation of Aboriginality!
MOLLY: Well, you are Aboriginal right?
GINNY: Yes, but I don't have one, Molly. I don't have one, okay?
MOLLY: Ooh, and if you don't have one that would make you seem like a liar.
GINNY: I know.
MOLLY: Like someone who used cultural stereotypes to lie to get what they want—
GINNY: / Yeah. Okay.
MOLLY: Like someone who lied about their culture to get into a company that's based on the authenticity of culture that's used to empower a whole race of / people.
GINNY: / Cool, Molly. You get it.

MOLLY: I think I can help.
GINNY: You can?
MOLLY: Yes but we have to go now, I just had an UberEats order come through!

GINNY *jumps on the handlebars and* MOLLY *pedals away.*

SCENE 8: HUMPEE BY BEACH

A bachelor pad humpee is set up by the beach. It's just off the busy boardwalk of the Gold Coast but to TRUE LOVE INTEREST *... it's home.*
TRUE LOVE INTEREST *appears, doing majestic 'Aboriginal' dancing.*
GINNY *is mesmerised. Everything turns slow motion. Doves fly behind them. It's love at first sight.*

GINNY: Who is that?!
MOLLY: He's the guy who's gonna help us. His name is True Love Interest. It's a bit of a giveaway, isn't it?
GINNY: What is?
MOLLY: His name.
GINNY: What do you mean?
TRUE LOVE INTEREST: Hey, looky-loo. I'm not dancing for free.

Holds out his busking cap.

MOLLY: I'm your cousin. I'm not paying to watch you dance. Also, I don't have any money. I'm Irish.
TRUE LOVE INTEREST: Molly, you're not Irish.
MOLLY: Yes I am.
TRUE LOVE INTEREST: The Irish fought the British colonisers like we did, sis! They're the Blacks of Europe!
MOLLY: Well they're the whites of here! So I'm white!
TRUE LOVE INTEREST: Molly, you've got a staunch Black man's blood running through your veins! Your dad started a tent embassy!
MOLLY: No he didn't! He worked at Tent World and he put up tents! In the tent section! Which was everywhere because it's Tent World! I'm not having this argument again. [*Whispering*] I'm after a confirmation.
TRUE LOVE INTEREST: Which one you want? I got everything. Noongars, Murris, Kooris, TIs. Half castes, full castes, short Blacks, long Blacks, Kinder Surprises. Which one you want?

MOLLY: [*to* GINNY] Which one?
TRUE LOVE INTEREST: This is for her?! Why would she need one? She's Black.
GINNY: Hey! I'm not white—wait—you think I'm Black?
TRUE LOVE INTEREST: Well, you are, aren't ya?
GINNY: But everyone always thinks I'm white!
TRUE LOVE INTEREST: Colonisation of the mind, bruh.
    Skin colour is a way whitefellas police and commodify Aboriginality. Like with these goddamn Confirmations.

    He spits.

I hate them so damn much.
GINNY: Then why are you selling them?
MOLLY: Don't get him started.
TRUE LOVE INTEREST: To destabilise the economic racial supremacy of white police-state bureaucracy.
GINNY: Really?
TRUE LOVE INTEREST: And I have a raging ice addiction.

    Beat.

Nah, gammon.
    I made some bad investments in Bitcoin.
GINNY: Oh yeah, that Bipt Coin!
TRUE LOVE INTEREST: You mean Bitcoin—
GINNY: Bipt Coin—
TRUE LOVE INTEREST *and* MOLLY: Bitcoin.
GINNY: Bipt.
TRUE LOVE INTEREST *and* MOLLY: Bit.
GINNY: Bipt.
MOLLY: [*whispering to* TRUE LOVE INTEREST] She was in a freak smoking accident.
TRUE LOVE INTEREST: Oooh okay.
    Look, I don't know why a beautiful Blaque Queen like yourself needs one of these dirty dogtags that uphold colonial definitions of Blackness therefore you're also upholding those values by participating in the system but hey, it's not my place to judge. This is the cost.

    TRUE LOVE INTEREST *hands* GINNY *a folded piece of paper.*

GINNY: I don't even have half of that!
MOLLY: We'll take it!
GINNY: Molly, I can't let you do that.
MOLLY: Ginny, as a white person, it's my turn to pay the rent.
TRUE LOVE INTEREST: Molly, you're not white and you don't have any money. You owe everyone money, including me! You don't have money 'pay back'.
GINNY: That's a bit of a racist stereotype isn't it, Aboriginal people not being good with money?
TRUE LOVE INTEREST: Molly isn't bad with money because she's Aboriginal. It's because she's a woman.
MOLLY: I'm not Aboriginal! I'm white now! Watch!

> MOLLY *starts River Dancing. She is terrible and a potato hits her.*

HECKLER: [*offstage*] Cut it out, cum face!
MOLLY: Joke's on them. I love potatoes.

> MOLLY *takes a big bite off the potato and forces it down with a smile.*

Deadly!
TRUE LOVE INTEREST: Ha! That's a Black word!
MOLLY: It's Irish! Just get the confirmation!

> TRUE LOVE INTEREST *exits.*

GINNY: I can't let you do this, Molly! I have nothing to pay you back with. Not until my dad dies and I inherit everything.
MOLLY: Ginny, I help you achieve your dream and you help me achieve mine.
GINNY: What is your dream?
MOLLY: I bet you were wondering why Chandon and Kyle were calling me Alinta? I used to be a Blaque Showgirl.
GINNY: What happened?
MOLLY: I left.
GINNY: Why would you do that?!
MOLLY: Because they wanted me to be someone I wasn't.
GINNY: Molly Meldrum?
MOLLY: No. What? No. Why would you even think that—anyway— My name used to be Alinta Allen. I was a Blaque Showgirl.

GINNY: What happened?
MOLLY: I left.
GINNY: Why in the flippety flip would you do that?

Throughout the following monologue MOLLY'*s Irish accent starts to drop as her lived experience is shared but goes back to Irish by the end.*

MOLLY: Ginny, I know it's your dream to be a Blaque Showgirl but being a Blaque Showgirl means you're Aboriginal and being Aboriginal in this country isn't a good thing, you should know that!

I hated always being followed around stores by security. Not being able to get a taxi or my Uber rating always being low even though I was always quiet and polite and never slammed the door!

Not getting approved for rentals. Or getting pulled over by police—even when I was just standing!

Always nervous when anything to do with Aboriginal people was brought up in case it was racist.

Not being able to watch morning TV in case there was a panel on 'Aboriginal dysfunction'. People always thinking I got free stuff or special treatment just because I was Aboriginal.

My family constantly suffering and dying from chronic health issues.

Kids being stolen.

Living in constant fear.

Never feeling safe.

Generation after generation of having no worth as a person in this country.

Aboriginal people die eight years before non-Aboriginal people and I didn't just want live longer, I wanted to live!

Live a life where I wasn't defined first and foremost by my race.

No-one ever saw 'Alinta'. They just saw an Aboriginal woman.

One day, when looking at a missing poster, I realised that white women get to be seen as individuals! When white women go missing or get murdered, they get called by their names and get their own posters! Alone!

Black women … it's always 'Aboriginal' first even if anyone notices or they just wait until enough of us die and then there's a march or hashtag and then … nothing.

When white women are angry, it's a reckoning. They get books and speaking tours!

When I was angry, I was a problem to be destroyed or worse … ignored.

And I was so so angry. So angry I couldn't just be the person I wanted to be. That being Aboriginal determined my value in every aspect of my life and I had no say in it!

None at all!

So being white … wow … it seemed incredible. So when I discovered I was white it was like a weight lifted off my shoulders. I mean, look at Confirmations—white people don't need them! So I tore mine up and I decided I wasn't going to suffer anymore. I was going to embrace my heritage, take my privilege and be white!

GINNY: You go girl!

MOLLY: But I was still dancing at Blaque Showgirls and it didn't feel right. I wanted to do the dances of *my* people. One day, during the TokenBlackfullaOnAPanel tap dance, I couldn't help it. I just … I went rogue. I started River Dancing to treaty. And that was the last time I saw Chandon and Kyle.

GINNY: What happened?

MOLLY: They pulled me offstage with one of those really long wooden sticks that are curved like a hook at the end.

GINNY: Wow! I didn't even those existed in real life!

MOLLY: Neither did I!

GINNY: So why do you need my help?

MOLLY: In BrisVegas, people still aren't exactly accepting of my River Dancing or me being white.

Blaque Showgirls is the most popular act in BrisVegas.

If you got into Blaque Showgirls maybe you could convince them to do a River Dancing act! I could do the guest spot and people will finally accept me as white!

GINNY: That sounds ambitious but tenuous, Molly.

MOLLY: We want similar things Ginny. To be accepted by our communities. To create change. To do what we love. You help me, I help you Ginny.

GINNY: Deal!

MOLLY *and* GINNY *do an Irish shake. With their legs.* TRUE LOVE INTEREST *enters.*

TRUE LOVE INTEREST: Here ya go, one confirmation. Signed by the One True White Elder—Andrew Bolt himself.

GINNY: Next stop: Blaque Showgirls!

TRUE LOVE INTEREST: Blaque Showgirls?! What do you want with Blaque Showgirls?!

GINNY: I'm gonna be one! The greatest Blaque Showgirl the world has ever seen!

TRUE LOVE INTEREST: Why would a pure Black girl like you wanna be part of that culture-destroying, sell-out, corporate cunt of a machine?

GINNY: How dare you! My mother was a Blaque Showgirl!

TRUE LOVE INTEREST: I'm sorry. But Blaque Showgirls is nothing but a minstrel show. Making our Blaque Queens sell our culture and sex to the white man. Look at Molly, they just chewed her up and spat her out!

MOLLY: They didn't chew me up and spit me out! They pulled me offstage with one of those long wooden sticks with a hook on it!

TRUE LOVE INTEREST: They don't exist anymore!

MOLLY: They do!

GINNY: But if I don't dance with Blaque Showgirls … How will I learn about my culture?

TRUE LOVE INTEREST: You wanna know pure cultural ways—you come dance with me sometime.

GINNY: With you … ?

TRUE LOVE INTEREST: With me. I'm from the Lublysing Tribe. Our culture is rich and stems back thousands and thousands of years. Dance with me and you'll know what it is to be Black.

GINNY: That's all I've ever wanted! Yes, True Love Interest! Yes!
    Why are you being so nice to me?

TRUE LOVE INTEREST: In this post colonial world, no-one appreciates what I have to give. I would've been a chief. I'm taking that power back. Decolonising BrisVegas. One Aboriginal woman at a time.
    I only ask one thing in return.

GINNY: What?

TRUE LOVE INTEREST: Are you a virgin?
GINNY: What?
TRUE LOVE INTEREST: Nah, gammon. But you give me everything you got, Ginny Jones. We train every morning by the beach. Traditional dance. Traditional way. Just like our ancestors would have.
And occasionally we'll do weddings.
GINNY: I'm in.

SCENE 9: MONTAGE

Success Montage to show how good GINNY*'s life is at the moment:*

GINNY *trains with* TRUE LOVE INTEREST. *He pushes her harder than she's ever been pushed before.*

GINNY *gets a makeover by* MOLLY. *She is sleeker with bigger hair and browner nipples than ever before. She wears Aboriginal Flag attire.*

GINNY *training and learning dances with* KYLE *and* CHANDON.

GINNY, MOLLY *and* TRUE LOVE INTEREST *Sit Around the Campfire.*

They eat a Kangaroo on a spit roast. They laugh and tell stories. MOLLY *does a jig and plays the fiddle.*

SCENE 10: HUMPEE BY THE BOARDWALK

TRUE LOVE INTEREST *is teaching* GINNY *but she messes up and* TRUE LOVE INTEREST *angrily stops dancing, moody.*

TRUE LOVE INTEREST: You're doing it all wrong, Ginny!
You're dancing with your arms!
And your feet!
And your torso!
You're dancing with your hand-eye coordination! Like an idiot!
GINNY: What else do I dance with?
TRUE LOVE INTEREST: Your heart, Ginny. Dance from the heart.
GINNY: I don't even know where my heart is!
TRUE LOVE INTEREST: In your body!
GINNY: But is it slightly to the left or slightly to the right?!

TRUE LOVE INTEREST *puts his hand on* GINNY*'s chest. They look at each other.*

TRUE LOVE INTEREST: It's here.
GINNY: But is that your left or my right?!
TRUE LOVE INTEREST: Just ask! Ginny, we've got the Cohen Bar mitzvah tomorrow night and you need to be ready!
GINNY: You're not helping!
TRUE LOVE INTEREST: What more do you want from me?!
GINNY: I DON'T ... Know.

> *Beat.*

I'm sorry.
I'm just so tired.
TRUE LOVE INTEREST: Maybe I'm being too hard on you.
GINNY: No. You're right. I feel something holding me back.
TRUE LOVE INTEREST: What is it?
GINNY: Fear.
TRUE LOVE INTEREST: What could a beautiful Black queen like you be scared of?
GINNY: These last few weeks have been the best of my life. Meeting you. Dancing. Being here. But I'm so scared.
TRUE LOVE INTEREST: Of what?
GINNY: You wouldn't understand! I'm not like you, True Love Interest.
    I didn't grow up with my mob ... I grew up in white bread, racist Chithole ...
TRUE LOVE INTEREST: Wasn't Chitole voted one of the most progressive towns in all of Australia?
GINNY: It's the home of racism! People constantly called me racist names, they tried to ban me from the local talent contest because I am Aboriginal. There was even this infamous crazy woman who was a vicious racist called Aryan Annie who was from there a very long time ago. Chitole isn't my home.
    Until now, I've never felt like I had a home! What if I lose this one?!
TRUE LOVE INTEREST: It must be so hard to not have a home or know your mob. Like a piece of you is missing.
GINNY: Like I don't have a place.
TRUE LOVE INTEREST: You poor thing.

> *Beat.*

Well I could tell you about ... No, I couldn't possibly.

GINNY: Tell me what?
TRUE LOVE INTEREST: No, I can't.
GINNY: You were going to say something!
TRUE LOVE INTEREST: Ginny, as much as I want to, sometimes you have to put others first, like my mob.
GINNY: What if one day I was *your* mob? Maybe I am now? Falling ... into your mob. Are you too?
TRUE LOVE INTEREST: ... Yes ... I think so ... falling deep in your ... mob.

They stare into each other's eyes.

There's a dance. A dance of my tribe. To be danced only by a chosen few. It's about finding your home.
The home inside of yourself.
It's a Sacred, Sacred Really Sacred Dance.
GINNY: What's it called?
TRUE LOVE INTEREST: The Sacred, Sacred Really Sacred Dance.
GINNY: Please teach me. Teach me how to dance. So I'll always ... I'll aways be home.
TRUE LOVE INTEREST: I'll do it on one condition.
Don't you ever show it to that Blaque Showgirls mob.
What I teach you—You don't share with them. Okay, Ginny?
GINNY: Okay.
TRUE LOVE INTEREST: [*sexily*] Because if you do ... my tribe ... they'll chop my dick off.
GINNY: [*sexily*] Is that like some kind of traditional punishment?
TRUE LOVE INTEREST: [*sexily*] No, its new. It was my idea, actually. To sort the alphas from the cucks.

> TRUE LOVE INTEREST *takes* GINNY's *hand and slowly starts doing beautiful, graceful dance moves. As the dance unfolds, they start to kiss.*

GINNY: It's raining.
TRUE LOVE INTEREST: I know.
GINNY: But we're inside.
TRUE LOVE INTEREST: My Blaque Queen, it's our ancestors. Crying at the beauty of our love.
GINNY: No, your roof's broken.

Beat.

BLAQUE SHOWGIRLS   31

TRUE LOVE INTEREST: So should I get a bucket or …
GINNY: FUCK THE BUCKET!

> GINNY *kisses* TRUE LOVE INTEREST *and they fall to the floor, in a squirming pile of bodies, and they make love under the rain.*

TRUE LOVE INTEREST: [*moaning*] Ginny … Ginny … Ginny … Oh, Ginny …

> AUNTY MAVIS *sits by the river knitting. The wind blows in the trees,* LEAVES *whisper in the wind:*

LEAVES: Ginnnnnny … ginnnyyyyyyy … ginnnnnnyyyyy …
AUNTY MAVIS: Ginny? Who the fuck is Ginny?

SCENE 11: CROWN CASINO GOLD

GINNY, CHANDON, KYLE *and* CLARINDA *are in rehearsals, practicing a dance.*

CHANDON: One and two, one and two, come on people, it's opening night! Get it right!

> *Suddenly* CLARINDA *screams and falls to the ground and screams!* KYLE *rushes to help.*

CLARINDA: Aaaargggh!
KYLE: What's wrong?
CLARINDA: It's Ginny's pink nipples. I can't work with them sticking out like that. One looked me straight in the eye and the other one tripped me over!

> KYLE *darts back and forth and up and down staring at* GINNY'S *nipples.*

GINNY: I'm sorry. The nipple-paint's come off. I don't know why it keeps happening.
CHANDON: Kyle, fix it.
KYLE: Ginny, give me a clearer look of your nipples.

> GINNY *sticks her pink nipples out and* KYLE *inspects them.*

Hmmm. Okay, I think I've figured it out. You have enlarged lactiferous ducts. That means your nipples are sucking up the paint. We'll fix you up with a good nipple primer to coat the ducts and create a barrier.

GINNY: Wow, you know so much about nipples.

KYLE: It's my job. My passion, really. Help Clarinda offstage then speak to props, say you need paint and primer.

> GINNY *helps* CLARINDA *hobble off stage as* CLARINDA *covers her eyes, refusing to look at* GINNY *nipples.*

CHANDON: What are we going to do?! Clarinda is one of the main dancers!

KYLE: Clarinda's camel toe has been ruining the show. The moot on that woman is greedy.

CHANDON: Opening night has to be perfect! The board will be there! We blow their minds, we get them fucked up at Cunty Mayo, and then BAM, hostile takeover!

KYLE: It's fine. We'll put in Ginny.

CHANDON: Ginny? No.

KYLE: Why not?

CHANDON: She's too … slow. She's half-step behind for the MootMoot Wet Wet Dance and doesn't get wide enough to the ground.

KYLE: A half step? You're the best dancer here. Surely you can fix that, right?

CHANDON: I could. Easily. I'm the star and it needs to be perfect.

KYLE: Sounds like you're afraid of a little competition?

CHANDON: I need all eyes on me tonight because I want to see the look in their eyes when they find out we won and realise just how much they have lost. That they don't own me anymore.

We have deal, Kyle.

KYLE: Then we need opening night to be perfect. You said so yourself. Ginny is going onstage. I'm making the call. I'll sign my shares when we open. You make sure the show is perfect. With Ginny in it. That's the deal.

> GINNY *re-enters with large tins of pain and brushes (like the kind from Bunnings).*

Ginny. I don't know what you've been doing these last few weeks, but your dancing … It's amazing. Congratulations, Ginny. You're ready. You'll on for opening night!

GINNY: I will?!

KYLE: Yes!

GINNY: Wait, that's tonight?
CHANDON: Kyle, she doesn't even know when opening night is!
KYLE: Why? You have plans, pink nips?
GINNY: No, not at all. I'm ready.
KYLE: Chandon is going to run through the dances with you and we'll get that nipple situation under control. Wouldn't want those pink piglets making an appearance on stage.
GINNY: Of course!
KYLE: See you after the show, Ginny. You'll be … deadly.

> KYLE *exits.* CHANDON *begins painting* GINNY*'s nipples, The rest of the scene play out very sexily between* CHANDON *and* GINNY*: a game of sexual thrill.*

CHANDON: There's a lot riding on tonight. Ginny. More than you can imagine.
GINNY: Thank you for putting me on Miss Connors.
CHANDON: Chandon.
GINNY: Chandon.
CHANDON: I was against putting you on opening night. I don't think you're ready but Kyle has a boner for your fair as snow puss-puss. It's his weakness.
GINNY: It's not like that.
CHANDON: I know Kyle like the back of my foot. It's exactly like that. This brown nipple requirement is so silly, don't you think?
GINNY: … I don't know.
CHANDON: Your pink nipples are fine. I like your pink nipples? Do you like your pink nipples?
GINNY: I like having nipples.
CHANDON: The board insists on brown nipples. See, they have this idea of what a Blaque Showgirl is. How we should look. Dance. Be. But Blaque Showgirls was created to celebrate Blaque Women, ALL Blaque women.
GINNY: Like my mum.
CHANDON: I've been at Blaque Showgirls a very long time. What was your mother's name?
GINNY: I … I … I don't know.

> GINNY *starts to cry. Sexily.*

My father never let us talk about her. All I have is the memory of her when I was a child and one single picture.

CHANDON: You'll have to show me her picture sometime. Maybe we can find her.

GINNY: Really?

CHANDON: Really.

GINNY: Why are you helping me?

CHANDON: Who says I am?

GINNY: Are you?

CHANDON: What's the saying … You keep your friends close but the cunts closer.

GINNY: Am I a friend or a cunt to you?

CHANDON focuses on finishing painting GINNY's nipples. Sexily.

CHANDON: Friends? Cute.

CHANDON pulls GINNY in close to her face.

You don't get to be queen of the pound without biting other bitches.

SCENE 12: CROWN CASINO GOLD / SHOWROOM

It is the night of Ginny's debut dance performance. The Crown Casino Gold Showroom stage is set.

Dance Sequence: The #SorryNotSorry Dance.

CHANDON and GINNY are totally in sync. The all of a sudden GINNY accidentally missteps and CHANDON's eye's glare with fury.

GINNY has no choice: she goes rogue and upstages upstage CHANDON. CHANDON gets pissed. They battle in the dance and go off routine.

Ends with GINNY on a chair, Flashdance-style, pulling on chains and buckets of water fall on them.

The word SORRY is lit up in fire behind them.

SCENE 13: CROWN CASINO GOLD / BACKSTAGE

GINNY *comes running offstage.*

MOLLY: Ginny! Oh, Ginny! You were so amazing! Everybody loved you! Like, they actually loved you. They were like, I love that girl. She can dance good.

GINNY: It was amazing! Molly, I've never felt so alive, so invigorated, so in touch with my people! Did my nipples look brown, Molly? Like the others? Did they?

MOLLY: Oh yes. They were very brown. Like corduroy. Or brown like bark. Or brown like rocks.

GINNY: Well I better take it off. I've got to go see True Love Interest. We're dancing at the Cohen's bar mitzvah!

MOLLY: I'll go get the mop!

GINNY: And the eBike!

> MOLLY *exits.* CHANDON *stalks over grabs* GINNY *between the crotch.*

CHANDON: You want a cigarette, Ginny?

GINNY: What?

CHANDON: I just thought you might want a cigarette after you fucked me? Because that's what you did! You fucked me out there, Ginny. You fucked me! Did you like it? Did it feel good, Ginny? It must've of because of how much you fucked me!

GINNY: Maybe you were just too slow, Chandon.

CHANDON: Excuse me?

GINNY: Isn't it like you said, you don't get to be Queen of the pound without biting other bitches.

CHANDON: You dirty little biscuit!

> KYLE *enters.*

KYLE: / Leave the little meat pie alone, Chandon.

CHANDON: Meat pie?

KYLE: Yes, Meat pie. White on the outside, brown on the inside. Filled with meat and juicy gravy ... with a bit of gristle. A bite no man can resist.

Ginny, you were brilliant. I've never seen any Blaque Showgirl debut like that before.

CHANDON: She fluked it! And then fucked it for me! She stepped into my light and then cut me off in the Abstudy Arabesque! And as if that wasn't enough fucking, she turned me over, stole my moment and fucked me some more! That's my moment! My bucket!

KYLE: Calm down Chandon, you're coming across a little ... angry.

CHANDON: Excuse me? Angry?!

> KYLE *pulls* CHANDON *aside to talk privately.* GINNY *pretends not to listen.*

KYLE: Look ... Chandon, why don't you take the night off?

CHANDON: I don't take nights off. Especially tonight.

KYLE: Chandon ... I'm sorry but the board only want to see Ginny tonight.

CHANDON: What?!

KYLE: This is a good thing! I'll butter them up tonight with Pink Nips and sign the shares over tomorrow.

> KYLE *walks back over to* GINNY.

Ginny, go put on some deodorant and I'll meet me out front! You're coming to Cunty Mayo with me and the board.

GINNY: But ... I ...

KYLE: But what?

GINNY: Nothing!

KYLE: Good! We're leaving now. Go! And use the chemical deodorant not that natural shit. Doesn't work. Not for you.

> GINNY *exits.* KYLE*'s phone starts ringing and he turns to leave.*

CHANDON: You're nothing but a butt boy, Kyle.

KYLE: Have you ever tried putting anything up your butt, Chandon? It feels good. Really good.

Check mate.

> KYLE *takes the call and exits.*

Chandon's Angry Dance:

> CHANDON *does an angry dance: we see her precision and style as she let's her fit of rage take over, destroying the entire dressing room. Everything flies everywhere.*

CHANDON: ARRRRRRGGGGGHHHHHHHHHH! THAT STUPID JOHNNY COME LATELY CUNT! I'LL GIVE YOU ANGRY BLACK WOMAN!!

Suddenly CHANDON *notices a photo tucked into the mirror, sitting neatly amongst the mess, labelled: Mum.* CHANDON *unfolds it and examines it.*

Wait … Wait a minute? Is this … Is this Ginny's mother?

CHANDON *laughs. Laughs some more. And more. Transition into* KYLE *and* GINNY *laughing.*

SCENE 14: CREAM OF CUNTY MAYO

GINNY *and* KYLE, *sit around laughing, drinking and taking drugs!*

KYLE: Oh man! Aren't the board great!

GINNY: They really are.

KYLE: A good group of men. Real men. White businessmen.

GINNY: I loved how they kept asking me where I'm from? And how Aboriginal I am? And what percentage? God, now I really feel like a real Blackfulla. A real Blaque Showgirl.

KYLE: Being a Blaque Showgirl is more than just winning an impromptu dance-off on opening night, Pink Nips.

But who knows, if she ever leaves, maybe you could be the new Chandon.

GINNY: I could be better than Chandon now. I was tonight.

KYLE: You've got moxy, Ginny. I'll give you that but Chandon has been at Blaque Showgirls since the start. She *is* Blaque showgirls. And she has big plans. A little too big but she gave me my start and I lost my belly button virginity to her, so I owe her some loyalty. That and Chandon knows a lot of secrets about me. So many secrets. Especially all the butt stuff. Oh no, I told someone again! Shit!

GINNY: It must be hard having someone boss you around like that all the time. Like they are in control of you.

KYLE: I'm the boss! I'm in control! See! Watch me to do this!

KYLE *does a karate kick, jump, some dance move that involves all his limbs or a cartwheel.*

I did that! See! I'm in control of me!
GINNY: Of course! Of course! That was so good! I mean, I didn't mean to imply that you don't look like a powerful man like the men of the board. You do. You look like you belong right beside them. I should know, my dad was on lots of boards. Have you ever wanted that?
KYLE: Your dad? I've never met him but sexuality is fluid—
GINNY: / I mean, wanted to be on the board of Blaque Showgirls. Not having to answer to Chandon or the board members because you would be their equal. One of them. A proper man.
KYLE: I've got nothing they want.
GINNY: You've got me.
KYLE: Listen up. Chandon brought us the Cheeky Bin Chook dance. The dance of her people. It had never been seen and now it's our most famous act.

Why should I put my neck on the line for you? What can you give us that no-one else has seen before?

Voices start swirling around in GINNY'*s head.*

GINNY *Voice Sequence:*

TRUE LOVE INTEREST: [*voiceover*] What I teach you, you don't share with that Blaque Showgirls mob.
CHANDON: [*voiceover*] You keep your friends close but cunts closer. You dirty, little biscuit!
TRUE LOVE INTEREST: [*voiceover*] You'll always be home … because you'll have a home inside yourself.
AUDIENCE: [*voiceover*] White Chocolate! White Chocolate! White Chocolate!
MOLLY: [*voiceover*] Diddly Dee, I love potatoes!
GINNY: I have a dance I can give you! It's a world exclusive.
KYLE: What dance?
GINNY: The Sacred Sacred Really Sacred Dance.
KYLE: The Sacred Sacred Really Sacred Dance?
GINNY: Yes.
KYLE: How did you get it? Who showed you?!
GINNY: It was passed down to me.
KYLE: I've been trying to get that dance for years. Years! It would make so much money! You're being real right now?

GINNY: As real as real can be.
KYLE: If you can give me this dance, Ginny, the board will promote me to Chair of the Board. I'll be rich forever. I won't have to answer to any Blaque women! I'll be a real man! A proper businessman! Amongst white businessmen!
GINNY: I'll only give you the Sacred, Sacred Really Sacred dance on one condition: You make me number one Showgirl.
KYLE: What?
GINNY: Replace Chandon with me. You get on the board and I'll the lead Blaque Showgirls.

> KYLE *Voice Sequence:*

CHANDON: [*voiceover*] We'll have the majority of shares and we can take over.
GINNY: [*voiceover*] A world exclusive!
MOLLY: [*voiceover*] Diddly dee! I'm white now!
CHANDON: [*voiceover*] We can take it slow with your belly button. Ease in.
TRUE LOVE INTEREST: [*voiceover*] We can just close our eyes and touch a little. Heterosexuality is a colonial construct.
CHANDON: [*voiceover*] We'll be our own bosses.
KYLE: Okay … I'll do it!
> Ginny! Oh Ginny! This will definitely get me in on the board with all those white businessmen! You're gonna make me so rich! So fucking rich!

> KYLE *does some more drugs.* KYLE *offers* GINNY *some drugs.*

Let's celebrate with drugs, Ginny! Here—do them! Do the drugs! DJ! Play your sexiest Irish song!

> GINNY *takes the drugs. As she does topless* RIVER DANCERS *and* LEPRECHAUNS *enter the room. Dancing and serving drinks.*

> *A party explodes around* KYLE *and* GINNY. *They take more drugs and cheer the dancers.*

> KYLE *and* GINNY *do a line of coke at the same time. As they sniff through rolled up notes down the table, their lines meet each other. Like in* The Lady and the Tramp *when they eat spaghetti and it's the same piece of pasta.*

GINNY *and* KYLE's *eyes meet. Suddenly they kiss.*

And kiss some more. Urgently.

KYLE *pushes the pile of coke off the table in one, swift arm movement.*

All of a sudden, KYLE *and* GINNY *are fucking. It's violent and coke-fuelled.*

It's like the pool sex scene in Showgirls.

The DANCERS *awkwardly leave—but not before filming some of it on their phones.*

SCENE 15: CREAM OF CUNTY MAYO / OUTSIDE

GINNY *walks out of the Cream of Cunty Mayo.* SMOKE BOMB! CHANDON *appears in an angry puff of smoke.*

CHANDON: Well if it isn't little ol' Ginny Jones.
GINNY: Ugh it's you.

    CHANDON *plays with the photo in front of* GINNY's *face.*

CHANDON: Sure you're not missing something?
GINNY: No.
CHANDON: You sure? You sure you're not missing … a photo perhaps?

    CHANDON *waves the photo in* GINNY's *face—*GINNY *realises!*

GINNY: The photo of my mum! Give it back!
CHANDON: You know, I've been around a lot longer than people give me credit for.
    Maybe it's my youthful looks. But I started dancing at Blaque Showgirls over fifty years ago before it was even Blaque Showgirls.
GINNY: Wait, how old are you?
CHANDON: None of your fucking business! I knew your mum.
GINNY: You did?
CHANDON: She was around right from the very start. I should burn this photo.
GINNY: Give me the photo of my mum!

    GINNY *keeps trying to get the photo back from her mum.*

CHANDON: Your mother was special. One of a kind. She tried to destroy me too.

GINNY: You were probably jealous!

CHANDON: Oh, I had a lot of feelings about your mother but jealousy wasn't one of them.

GINNY: Give it back!

CHANDON: See … *Ginny Jones* … We faced a lot of opposition when we first started. Now people travel from all over the world to see Blaque Showgirls. But back then, a lot people didn't want a bar of us. They were threatened. Scared. Prejudiced. They would call us 'dancing Abo's', 'big ol' boongs' /

GINNY: / What people?

CHANDON: Racist people. Like your mother.

GINNY: But she was a Blaque Showgirl!

CHANDON: Your mother wasn't a Blaque Showgirl! She was a white supremacist!

GINNY: No! You're lying! You're lying!

CHANDON: Your mother was Aryan Annie! The racist Aryan Annie!

GINNY: Then explain why she's dressed as a Blaque Showgirl?! Explain her beautiful Black, Black shiny skin! Her big, bursting beautiful red lips! Her very white, bright round eyes! Her big grin and white palms waving happily!

> GINNY *grabs the photo and pushes it in* CHANDON*'s face: it's a very clear photo of a woman in blackface.*

CHANDON: She's in blackface, you idiot. That's how she'd protest our shows! Mocking us in blackface!

GINNY: It's not true. She loved Aboriginal dancing!

CHANDON: She hated Aboriginal people and our dancing.

The irony. Her own daughter a Blaque Showgirl. Just as ironic as the way she died.

GINNY: She died in a sacred smoking ceremony!

CHANDON: She died from protesting a smoking ceremony and her black flammable face paint caught fire, exploding and burning her to the ground and killing everyone around her!

GINNY: That's impossible! I was there! It didn't affogatoo me at all! AFFOGATOO ME AT ALL!

CHANDON *walks closer towards* GINNY. *Yelling at* GINNY.

CHANDON: You are never going back onto that stage! You're never going to be a Blaque Showgirl! Never! Over my dead body—

All of a sudden MOLLY *comes speeding out of nowhere on her eBike.*

MOLLY: DIDDLY DEE!

CHANDON: ARGHHHH!

GINNY *seizes the opportunity and pushes* CHANDON *in front of* MOLLY. MOLLY *screeches on the breaks and beeps her horn, but it's too late. The eBike runs* CHANDON *over with a couple of loud thumps.* KYLE *comes running out of Cunty Mayo.*

KYLE: Someone call an amblience! Ginny, what happened?!

GINNY: Molly.

MOLLY: No, Ginny threw Chandon under the / eBike—

GINNY: / Molly hit Chandon! She was driving too fast and too dangerously because she's … Aboriginal … and a criminal! Someone call the police!

MOLLY: No, I didn't! That's a racist violent stereotype and I'm / white!

GINNY: / Yes, you did! You killed Chandon! Not me! You!

KYLE: I don't care! Ding Dong the bitch is dead!

KYLE *pulls* GINNY *in for a kiss as* CHANDON *lays on the road. Police arrive.* MOLLY *is taken away in handcuffs.*

SCENE 16: STREET

Front of newspaper: GINNY *now the Headliner for Blaque Showgirls. Wearing* GINNY *merch! Street spruiker! Like a vivid merch seller!*

MERCH BOY: Extra! Extra! Read all about it! Blaque Showgirls presents, in her first starring role, Ginny Jones featuring the Sacred, Sacred Really Sacred Dance. A world exclusive!

TRUE LOVE INTEREST *dances by and sees the picture of* GINNY: *he grabs his dick!*

TRUE LOVE INTEREST: Wait what?!

MERCH BOY: Ginny Jones is doing a world exclusive with the Sacred, Sacred Really Sacred Dance!

TRUE LOVE INTEREST: Since when?!
MERCH BOY: Since whenever! What about a glowstick for a hundred dollars?
TRUE LOVE INTEREST: No! No! This can't be happening! How did it happen?
MERCH BOY: Look man, I just sell merch. My real job is playing keys. Wanna buy a shirt or not?

SCENE 17: CROWN CASINO GOLD / BACKSTAGE

GINNY *sits backstage looking glamorous and beautiful, every bit the modern Blaque Showgirl. She has finally reached the top.*

A STAGEHAND *runs in with a headset.*

STAGEHAND: It's five minutes before you're needed onstage.
GINNY: Okay, sure, I'll be ready, thank you.
STAGEHAND: Break a leg, Ginny.
GINNY: Who?
STAGEHAND: You …
GINNY: Oy yeah, Sorry. Nerves.

> *Stagehand exits.* GINNY *looks into the mirror and reaches out to touch her face.*

Who am I?

> AUNTY MAVIS *pops up on the other side of the mirror, confused about where she is and being in a mirror.*

AUNTY MAVIS: Where am I? What's going on? Oh no, not you, Sarah Jane.
GINNY: Aunty Mavis!
AUNTY MAVIS: God, why you gotta choose to talk to me for. I was in the middle of bingo /
GINNY: / Is it true about my mother?
AUNTY MAVIS: It's true, Sarah Jane. Your mother was a famous blackface racist.
GINNY: Why didn't you tell me?!
AUNTY MAVIS: Oi! This isn't my fault! I tried to, Sarah Jane, but you don't / listen!
GINNY: / I thought she was a Blaque Showgirl! I thought I was finally a Blaque Showgirl like her.

AUNTY MAVIS: Wait … You're a Blaque Showgirl?
GINNY: I'm the lead.
AUNTY MAVIS: Christ Almighty, Sarah Jane! How'd that happen?!
GINNY: I'm so confused! I have people telling me I'm Black, people telling me I'm white—
AUNTY MAVIS: / Wait there—who's telling you you're Black?
GINNY: I feel like I don't know who I am anymore, Aunty Mavis.
AUNTY MAVIS: You need to tell the truth, Sarah Jane. You need to come clean. You've got to be honest.

 KYLE *suddenly walks into the room, overhearing the conversation.*

You're not Black, Sarah Jane. You never were.
KYLE: You're not Black?!
AUNTY MAVIS: I got to go now, Sarah Jane. Good luck with everything hey.
GINNY: No Aunty! Don't go!
AUNTY MAVIS: How the fuck do I get out of this fucking thing?
KYLE: What do you mean you're not Black?! Why was that woman calling you Sarah Jane?!
GINNY: That's my real name. Sarah Jane Jones. I made Ginny up. And … And …
KYLE: And what?!
GINNY: My mum wasn't Aboriginal. And neither am I.
KYLE: Fuck fuck fuck. Ginny, why'd you have to tell me this?
GINNY: I didn't do it on purpose!
KYLE: That doesn't make it any less bad! What the fuck am I going to do? We have millions riding on this show. This definitely counts as a fuck up. The board will kill me. We made a blood oath and if I break it, they'll cut my dick off and kill me dead!

 Okay, Ginny, let's just pretend you didn't tell me anything and you can just go onstage and dance. Give the audience and the board what they want.

 TRUE LOVE INTEREST *comes rushing in.*

TRUE LOVE INTEREST: Ginny … thank god, it's not too late.
 Listen to me—you can't do the dance. You can't!
GINNY: But I have to!
TRUE LOVE INTEREST: If you do the dance, my tribe will disown me.

GINNY: Maybe you shouldn't have taught me to the dance if you didn't want me to do it!
TRUE LOVE INTEREST: You promised!
GINNY: I actually didn't!
TRUE LOVE INTEREST: Don't you get it! Not only will they disown me, they'll punish me. They'll chop my dick off with a rock. And I love my dick. I love it. I don't want them to chop it off. It's really nice, it bends to the left and it has a vein! A nice hearty vein! And a long snout, like an anteater. Oh God, I never should've thought up the dick chopping. What was I thinking?!! Ginny, if you love me, please don't ever do the Sacred, Sacred Really Sacred Dance. Promise me. Ginny.
KYLE: No, Ginny! You can't! You have to do it! My dick! They'll chop it off!
TRUE LOVE INTEREST: My dick! They'll chop it off! You have to do it!
TRUE LOVE INTEREST *and* KYLE: My dick! My dick! No! My dick!

    KYLE *and* TRUE LOVE INTEREST *start to have a fight.* GINNY *screams 'No' and 'More'.*

GINNY: Shut up! Shut up! Both of you!
    I'm sick of all you Black people telling me what to do!
    Telling me what I am and what I'm not.
    How can you expect me to abide by your rules when you don't even know your rules.
    I am a woman. A woman just trying to find herself.
    All I want to do is dance.

    KYLE *knocks* TRUE LOVE INTEREST *out and* GINNY *runs onto stage.*

SCENE 18: CROWN CASINO / ON STAGE

GINNY *gets into position on stage. The show starts: the lights and sound begins.*

Her heart beats hard.

AUDIENCE: [*voiceover*] White Chocolate! White Chocolate! White Chocolate!

She rises into the spotlight and then suddenly CHANDON *rushes onto stage on bedazzled crutches with* MOLLY, *in a comical prison outfit (you know those old-timey ones) following after her.*

CHANDON: Stop the show! Stop the show!
    This woman isn't who you think she is!
GINNY: Chandon! Molly! What are you doing here?
CHANDON: Why the fuck do you think we're here?!
MOLLY: To expose you! Chandon bailed me out!
CHANDON: This woman isn't Aboriginal! Not one bit! She's a liar!

CHANDON walks over and pulls off GINNY's brown nipples, revealing pink nipples underneath.

The crowd gasps.

GINNY: Chandon is right. I didn't mean to lie to you all! But Kyle McLachlan told me I had to go onstage and pretend to be Aboriginal—otherwise the board would kill him.
KYLE: [*voiceover*] No! She told me she was Black from the start! No! No! NO! My dick!

Murder sounds. Blood splatters across the stage.

GINNY: I kind of thought he was exaggerating … but I guess not.
CHANDON: A white woman can't dance in Blaque Showgirls!
MOLLY: That's true! They pulled me offstage with a long wooden stick with a hook on the end!

Crowd gasps.

CHANDON: You're out, bitch! You're white and this is Blaque Showgirls. You have no place here.

GINNY: You're right. I'm sorry for lying, it was never my intention. I can't perform the Sacred, Sacred Really Sacred Dance. Not just because I'm white but because it's a dance about finding your home. And I don't have a home. I've never really had a home … not in Chitole … not here … not the island my father owns just off the coast or any of his other investment properties … I'm just a poor little white girl … with a dead white mother … trying to find a white place in a big Black world.

Inspirational music plays as GINNY *has an epiphany!*

GINNY: Wait a minute. I'm white!
I'M WHITE!
Of course I have a home!
My ancestors were brave explorers! Who travelled the world and made their home anywhere they wanted! Bringing with them wonderful gifts, like flour, sugar, iPhones!
You know what I've learned from my people?
Home isn't where you're born, it's where you make it.
That's what my ancestors did.
So I say my home is here, at Blaque Showgirls.
And if you tell me I can't dance here just because I wasn't born Black … Then you know what that is?
Racism.
The worst kind of racism.
Reverse-racism.

Applause from the crowd. GINNY *bows. A distant rumbling, growing louder.*

CHANDON: Wait … do you feel that? IT'S THE BOARD!

THE BOARD *enter in all their glory: It's a white guy with slightly woke vibes but capitalist rich person, always on his phone. Basically it's Kendall Roy.*

THE BOARD: Yo! Look, I don't want to take up too much space … But Kyle McLachlan's position has been vacated. I hate to be 'the man' here but we've been really worried about how monocultural and exclusive this show is: it needs more diversity. Our First Nations people should be embraced and their culture should celebrated by all of us. Blaque Showgirls for everybody.

CHANDON: No, that isn't why we started Blaque Showgirls at all!
THE BOARD: Times have changed. We need to tackle the real obstacles, like gender and class.
 And we think a woman as our new CEO AND board member would be amazing.
CHANDON: Yes!
THE BOARD: What?
CHANDON: You're talking about me right?
THE BOARD: Maybe one day when you're ready for it. But good for you for aiming high. But for now … Ginny, we want that woman person … To be you.
CHANDON: This is white supremacy!
GINNY: It's feminism in action!
THE BOARD: Our decision was based entirely on merit. Ginny is the best dancer in the show.
CHANDON: She's only been in the show one night!
THE BOARD: Do you accept, Ginny?
GINNY: I'll do it on two conditions.
 One. You don't have be Black to be a Blaque Showgirl anymore. Because aren't we all Indigenous to earth?
 Two. I've worked so hard to get here and now that I'm here, I'm going to share my platform. I want Chandon to be my co-star. Both of us. Our name in lights. Together. Like sisters.
THE BOARD: The Board accept your conditions.
GINNY: So, what do you say, Chandon? Will you be my co-star, sis?
CHANDON: No! Of course not! I should be fucking running it—not dancing in it with you! Am I the only person who see's anything wrong with this?
MOLLY: I do a bit.
 What about our deal, Ginny?
GINNY: What about it?
MOLLY: Your promise to let me dance?
GINNY: Sure! You can be a Blaque Showgirl again! If Chandon doesn't want to be co-star, you can!
MOLLY: And River Dance?
GINNY: Look, Molly, I don't think it's going work. Blaque Showgirls is about celebrating Blaque culture authentically. And you doing River Dancing isn't exactly … authentic … is it?

You're not white. You're pretending to be someone you're not. Denying your Aboriginality. I don't want to enable that kind of racism.

CHANDON: You're the racist! Your mother is responsible for the deaths of many Aboriginal people.

GINNY: I'm so sick of hearing that! 'You mother did this, she did that, she set fire to Aboriginal people.' It's in the past! You can't keep punishing me for it! Why should I be responsible for what my mother did?

CHANDON: Fine. You win, Ginny. Or Sarah Jones. Or whatever your name is. I tried my best and you still won. I had a plan. I was going to do a hostile takeover: become majority shareholder, put Kyle as chair, become CEO and then fill the board with First Nations women. I was going to start a whole new era of Blaque Showgirls: starring, run and owned by Black Women.

Now this show will just be you and a bunch other dickheads, blackfishing like a Kardashian, fetishisising stereotypes to make a buck.

But why I should I be surprised. It's all you've ever done.

You're dreams came true Ginny. You are a Blaque Showgirl. And you are exactly like your mother. You win.

CHANDON *begins to crutch off with defeat but a pesky piece of paper hits* CHANDON *in the face as she leaves. She shoos it away. The paper comes back this time and refuses to leave.*

Go away! Shoo!
Wait … what is this?

CHANDON *unfolds the pesky piece of paper.*

… Kyle's will!

[*Reading*] In the event of his death due to unforeseen circumstances or the unfortunate outcome of a blood oath gone wrong—all shares in the Blaque Showgirls will go to Chandon Connors.

He left his shares to me.
He did care.
So if my math is correct /

THE BOARD: / You know math?!

CHANDON: This means I now own the majority of Blaque Showgirls! Me! I'm the boss!

THE BOARD: No?!

CHANDON: Yes! I can take Blaque Showgirls back! I can do the plan! You're all fucking fired! All of you! Every single fucking one of you.

THE BOARD: You can't do this! It isn't fair!

CHANDON: This is your game. Your rules.

THE BOARD: We're not the real racists here! We spent years dedicated to helping you people!

CHANDON: Help?! You profited from us!

THE BOARD: We just wanted to help you people. Our vulnerable First Nations people.

CHANDON: We're not yours! We're ours! And you don't want to help, you want to be in charge.

THE BOARD: How dare you treat us like this after everything we've done for you. We were good to you! You would be nowhere without us! We built this show with you!

CHANDON: It was never yours! It wasn't meant for you! It was always for us!

Blaque Showgirls was created for Blaque women, every Blaque Woman, to come and be celebrated in a world that refuses to see them as people.

Black Women who are the scariest threats because we can never be a white man, not even close.

Black Women whose success is deemed as a threat.

Black Women whose labour is expected but never considered success.

Black Women whose voices are deemed less or too disruptive to have worth.

Black women who are either Aunty or Gins, Sluts or Victims, Angry or Silent, invisible or targeted, excellent or vilified.

Black Women who aren't included in Black or white history.

Black Women whose self empowerment is seen as radical because how dare they try to be more than what the world thinks they are.

Black Women who are tough and strong, who fight for their families and take the brunt of the violence the world throws.

Black Women who are sexual and in control, who have created and nurtured life and family on this continent for thousands of years.

Black Women whose love and laughter gives us light when the world is dark.

Blaque Showgirls is for the 'you've got an Aboriginal nose' and the 'you're so lucky you don't have your Dad's nose'.

For the 'Black bitch' 'Abo slut' and 'We don't have that shade of make-up'.

For the 'Are you sure you're Aboriginal' and the 'You're too light but I know you ain't white'.

For the 'You don't sound Black' and the 'Can you Black it up?'

For the 'You're pretty for an Aboriginal' and the 'Aboriginal women look like apes'.

For the 'They all sniff petrol' and 'You're different from the other ones'.

For the 'Black sluts' and 'Black cunts'.

For the 'You all used to live in humpees' and the 'You wouldn't even be here if it wasn't for whites'.

For the skinny ankles and big bums and bigger hearts and bigger minds.

For Black Women who are magic because they are future. Blaque Showgirls is for them. Because if this world ever changes for the better, it's because Black women pulled the fucking trigger!

[*To* THE BOARD] So please fuck off now.
Gorn. Fuck off.

CHANDON *shoos* THE BOARD *away with fucks as the* THE BOARD *leave.*

Molly, I'm sorry I didn't believe in you and had you pulled offstage with a long wooden stick with a hook on the end. I was so caught up in trying to take control of Blaque Showgirls from the white man that I forgot why we started Blaque Showgirls. So go live your dream, Molly. River dance your heart out. Take up all the space.

MOLLY: I don't think that's my dream anymore. I'm kinda shit at it and I'm sick of being hit by potatoes. Also, all the carbs aren't great for my diabetes.

I think I wanted to be white to feel like my own person. With value and freedom and choice. But I'm not going to find it by pretending to be white. I have a new dream, I think. I want to create a space that rejects colonialism and disrupts the norm. I mean, it doesn't transform structural inequalities but it creates space. And in space, radical moments can happen. I think that's my dream.

CHANDON: Wow, that's really smart.

MOLLY: It's in blood, my dad started a tent embassy. At the tent store. Tentworld.

What's your dream, Chandon?

CHANDON: You know … no-one has ever asked me so I haven't really given it a lot of thought. I've had goals … but they were always about needs, never about possibility. But I do know this: whatever our dreams are Molly … they're ours and they can be whatever the fuck we want them to be.

CHANDON and MOLLY begin to leave.

GINNY: What do I do now?

CHANDON: I forgot you were still here?

MOLLY: Why the fuck are you asking us?

CHANDON: Gorn then, White Chocolate. You're centre stage. It's all yours.

CHANDON and MOLLY exit.

Beat.

A chant from the audience gets louder and louder, creeping up on GINNY.

AUDIENCE: [*voiceover*] White Chocolate! White Chocolate! White Chocolate!

Irish music starts to play and GINNY reluctantly starts River Dancing.

And then she gets pulled off the stage with a long wooden stick with a hook at the end of it.

SCENE 19: STAGE—CODA

NARRATOR: [*voiceover*] In the dream time ... Right here ... right now ... We present ... not for your viewing pleasure, not for your gaze or commodification ... but start the applause because you are fucking blessed to see it ... because when the most vulnerable, least valued people in world get to th dream ... it creates limitless dreams for the rest of us ... It is ... Blaque Women Doing Whatever the Fuck They Want!

The incredible Women of the cast are lit up on stage.

The words BLAQUE WOMEN DOING WHATEVER THE FUCK THEY WANT lights up behind them.

Music plays. They're joined by the rest of the cast.

And everyone does whatever the fuck they want.

THE END

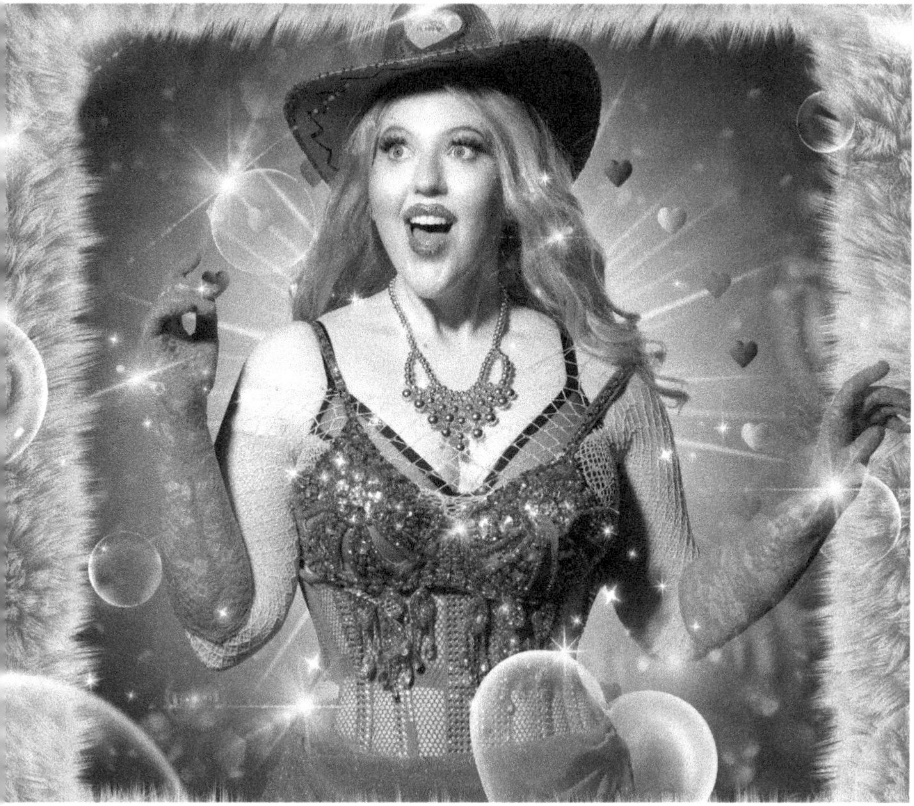

GRIFFIN THEATRE COMPANY PRESENTS

BLAQUE SHOWGIRLS

BY NAKKIAH LUI

4 SEPTEMBER – 14 OCTOBER 2023 | SBW STABLES THEATRE

GRIFFIN THEATRE COMPANY

Government partners

We would not be where we are today without the vision and generosity of the Seaborn, Broughton & Walford (S,B&W) Foundation, to whom we owe the great privilege of being able to perform in the much-loved SBW Stables Theatre.

CAST & CREATIVES

Co-Director **Shari Sebbens**

Co-Director **Ursula Yovich**

Set & Costume Designer **Cris Baldwin**

Lighting Designer **Verity Hampson**

Composer & Sound Designer **Jessica Dunn**

Choreographer **Sani Townson**

Intimacy Coordinator **Chloë Dallimore**

Voice & Accent Coach **Nick Curnow**

Community Engagement Lead **Neville Williams Boney**

Stage Manager **Isabella Kerdijk**

With
Mathew Cooper
Jonathan Jeffrey
Matty Mills
Angeline Penrith
Stephanie Somerville

Bloque Showgirls is supported by NIDA.

Ursula Yovich's role as Co-Director is generously supported by Rosemary Hannah & Lynette Preston.

PLAYWRIGHT'S NOTE

I wrote *Blaque Showgirls* in 2015 when people still called me an 'emerging playwright'. I prefer the term 'crowning playwright' because my work was screaming, new, and wrapped in a metaphorical secretion.

Blaque Showgirls is loosely inspired by the classic film *Showgirls*. The idea for it came from a place of spite, which, I'm unashamed to say, is a driver for much of my work.

I was constantly getting asked if I was interested in doing an adaptation of a 'classic', which was usually code for a play by a dead White man. It was less of a question and more of a direction: that adapting a 'classic' would cement my validity as a 'proper' playwright... not just an 'Aboriginal playwright'.

I remember being asked by a well-meaning White benefactor if the next step for me would be to write a play with White characters. Like that would be levelling up. I had coffee with the White head of an arts organisation who asked me why no Aboriginal playwright had written 'The Great Native Title Play?' I was told that 'White playwrights had given up space but no Black writers have stepped up.'

It was a confusing time. I was a crowning Black playwright, and the one thing I could see from all these people's opinions was that I wasn't what an Aboriginal writer was meant to be or should be. I definitely wasn't 'it', but they still defined me entirely by 'it'.

So when I was being asked to do an adaptation I rebelled by pitching a version of *Showgirls* that would interrogate the race and the performance and authenticity of voice.

Which was clearly where I was at.

Revisiting the text of *Blaque Showgirls* now feels like reading an entirely different writer: she's rousing, blunt, aggressively stupid with her jokes, fun and seemingly unafraid. I like her. I'm very cautious to make sure I'm not overwriting her.

I do not only feel incredibly lucky to have had the opportunity to revisit *Blaque Showgirls* but in a way, it has been healing.

I used to refer to the original production of *Blaque Showgirls* as a tragedy. It ended very differently. That end felt very true to when I wrote it. I wanted to use the extreme silly satire of the Sexploitation genre to mirror the ridiculousness of White Supremacy and say a very simple truth: White Supremacy continues to win.

And we see this every day: from sacred sites being blown up, people continuing to die in custody at the hands of thugs, to our humanity being debated and used as fodder in culture wars. I've felt this everyday of my life: from losing loved ones to racism to feeling like I have no worth in this country built on colonialism, no matter how successful my career is. I've felt that very much the last couple of years.

I wrote a letter to myself on my phone after the play debuted at Malthouse Theatre. I added to it after my play, *Blackie Blackie Brown* (which I see as a sequel to this show), came out. It was a list of reasons of why I write, who I write for and why I write for them.

As I was rewriting this play, I kept looking back at that letter to myself and I realised that whilst it interrogates tragedy, it doesn't have to end in tragedy. It can end the same way the play started: from spite and anger and the freedom that comes from being able to laugh as rebellion.

PLAYWRIGHT'S NOTE

It has felt like that writer from 2015 is reaching out to me from the past to tell me it's okay to be angry. I've done good. That I'm going to be okay. To keep going. All you need is one radical moment to keep going, to keep dreaming of a possibility for change.

This play is a love letter to all the people in my life who continue to create hope as a form of resistance. Who laugh in the face of oppression. Who rebel through love and dreaming.

I want to thank the cast and creatives of the premiere Malthouse season who helped build this work from its original production.

I cannot thank the amazing cast and creatives of this production who have brought this play to life enough. The generosity of the team at Griffin Theatre Company. A huge thanks to **Shari Sebbens** and **Ursula Yovich** for leading the way. And a special thanks to **Declan Greene** who was my first theatre friend and who continues to laugh at all my bad jokes.

Thank you to my family who are my constant dramaturgs with their wisdom and spirit. Thank you to my husband Gabe, my silver lining of colonisation, and my bubba, Lux, who is light.

Nakkiah Lui
Playwright

CO-DIRECTORS' NOTE

Co-directing this play is a lot of chaos. But it makes sense.

We, **Shari Sebbens** and **Ursula Yovich**, have never worked together before, save for one TV show where we had one scene together and our characters didn't even talk to each other. So to work together on **Nakkiah Lui**'s *Blaque Showgirls* has been an absolute pleasure. It's been a wonderful process of having ideas and bouncing them off each other, then trying them out with actors.

A term we're really fond of is 'lateral leadership'. As blackfulla creatives, we want to avoid a hierarchical sense in the room. It means you learn from the people next to you— it's not necessarily this top-to-bottom thing. It's getting to look to your peers and the actors—everyone! In that way, our process of rehearsing this play has felt truly collaborative.

There are so many levels of experience within the rehearsal room for this play. There are people who have been around for a long time, and there are people who have been around for a long time and haven't been given the *opportunity* to practise their craft. So the thing that we're most excited by is this cast of five Blak actors who are giving it their all everyday, taking up the most mad offers from us and making the maddest offers of their own. It's a reminder that actually, for people of colour, for Indigenous mob, blackfullas, the process is the product. Creating a room that is safe and supported and empowered and joyous, that's the product for us. Whatever ends up on stage is still very important, but for us, the journey that got us there is as vital as the end result.

Nakkiah's writing is full of comedy, full of satire. She's always pushing the envelope. We love that she goes there and you as the audience get to go with her. In the room, a lot of our joy has come from finding out how far we can push her comedy but still keeping the underlying message. Nakkiah's writing isn't silliness for the sake of silliness. There is something else that drives the whole piece. There is so much room to play. There are five to eight jokes per page, which is kind of mad to be able to inject that much humour, that much comedy, into a production. Yet the politics, for us anyway, always feel so clear and so present. The crucial thing for the audience of *Blaque Showgirls* to see is blackfullas existing in joy and laughter and silliness in ways that for so many decades white writers have never afforded us.

Nakkiah writes for us, but she also writes for herself... But then it becomes for every black woman, every blackfulla, every aunty, every uncle, every cousin brother—it becomes for everyone.

Shari Sebbens & Ursula Yovich
Co-Directors

BIOGRAPHIES

NAKKIAH LUI
PLAYWRIGHT

Nakkiah Lui is a writer/actor/director and Gomeroi/Torres Strait Islander woman. She began her playwriting career in 2013 with her first play, *This Heaven* (Belvoir St Theatre) and since then she has worked with every major theatre company in Australia. In 2012, Nakkiah was the inaugural recipient of both The Dreaming Award from The Aboriginal and Torres Strait Island Arts Board of the Australia Council and the Balnaves Foundation Indigenous Playwright Award. In 2018, Nakkiah was the recipient of the Patrick White Playwrights Fellowship at Sydney Theatre Company. In 2019, Nakkiah Lui was a winner of the NSW Premiers Literary recipient of the Nick Enright Playwriting Prize. In 2021, she was the recipient of the Russell Prize for Humour Writing for her play *Black is the New White* (Sydney Theatre Company).

Nakkiah is an AACTA and Logie nominated writer and actor. She was an actor/writer/director/producer of the ground-breaking series, *Black Comedy*, which ran for four seasons from 2014-2019. From then she went on to create/writer/star in the award-winning series, *Kiki & Kitty* which aired on ABC in 2017. Most recently, Nakkiah has been the co-creator/showrunner/star of the upcoming series, *Preppers*, as well contributing to a number of Australian and international drama and comedy series, such as *Total Control* and *The Great*.

Nakkiah has been a regular guest on ABC's *Q&A*, *The Drum* and Channel Ten's *The Project* as well as contributing to *The Guardian, New York Times* and a variety of other news outlets. Nakkiah is the co-host and co-creator of the award-winning podcast series, *Pretty for an Aboriginal* and Walkley Award nominated *Debutante* with Miranda Tapsell. In 2020, Nakkiah teamed with Australia's largest independent book publisher, Allen and Unwin to launch her own imprint, *JOAN*.

More recently, Nakkiah is currently under an overall deal with HBO in which she exclusively writing television for them and has just released her latest podcast for Audible Australia, *First Eat*.

SHARI SEBBENS
CO-DIRECTOR

Shari is a resident artist at Sydney Theatre Company. In 2018, she was named the Richard Wherrett Fellow. 2020 saw Shari mark her directional debut with *Superheroes* for Griffin. Since then, her directing credits include: for Black Swan State Theatre Company/Sydney Theatre Company: *City of Gold*; for Darlinghurst Theatre Company: *seven methods of killing kylie jenner* (co-directed with Zindzi Okenyo); for Melbourne Theatre Company/Sydney Theatre Company: *Is God Is* (co-directed with Zindzi Okenyo); for Sydney Theatre Company: *The 7 Stages of Grieving*, *Fences*. Shari's acting credits in theatre include: for Griffin: *The Bleeding Tree*; for Griffin/Queensland Theatre: *City of Gold*; for Griffin/La Boite: *A Hoax*; for Belvoir: *Back at the Dojo*, *Radiance*; for Black Swan State Theatre Company: *Our Town*; for Darwin Festival: *Wulamanyuwi and the Seven Pamanui*; for Queensland Theatre: *An Octoroon*; for Sydney Theatre Company: *A Cheery Soul*, *Black is the New White*, *The Battle of Waterloo*. Shari's film credits include: *Australia Day*, *The Darkside*, *The Moogai*, *The Sapphires*, *Teenage Kicks*, *Thor: Ragnarok* and *Top End Wedding*. Her television credits include: for ABC: *8MMM Aboriginal Radio*, *Black Comedy*, *The Gods of Wheat Street*, *The Heights*, *Redfern Now* (for which she was awarded the Logie Award – Graham Kennedy Award for Most Outstanding New Talent); and for Amazon Prime: *The Office*. Shari trained in Aboriginal Theatre at WAAPA and graduated from NIDA with a Bachelor of Fine Arts (Acting).

URSULA YOVICH
CO-DIRECTOR

Ursula is a proud Burarra and Serbian woman. A singer-songwriter, playwright, director and actor, Ursula has become one of Australia's most celebrated performers and has impressed audiences around the world, from the Queen Elizabeth Hall in London to Carnegie Hall in New York and the Concert Hall of the Sydney Opera House. She has had an extensive career in television, film and stage. Her television credits as an actor include: for ABC: *The Code*, *The Gods of Wheat Street*, *Preppers*, *Mystery Road*, *Redfern Now*, *Rake*; for Foxtel: *The Twelve*; and for Netflix/Peacock: *Irreverent*. She has also appeared in the films *Around the Block*, *Australia*, *Jindabyne* and *Top End Wedding*. Ursula is also an accomplished voice artist, lending her voice to children's TV series *Little J and Big Cuz*. She has received glowing reviews for her many theatrical roles and was awarded a Helpmann Award in 2007 for her performance in *Capricornia* for Company B Belvoir. In 2012, Ursula played to standing ovations for every single performance and a sold-out season for *The Barefoot Divas* as part of Sydney Festival. She also featured in Deborah Cheetham's *Pecan Summer*, Australia's first Indigenous opera. In 2019, she was nominated for the Nick Enright Prize for Playwriting in 2019 for her original rock musical *Barbara and the Camp Dogs*, which she co-wrote with Alana Valentine and starred in, and for which she received Best Female Lead in a Musical, Best Musical and Best Original Score at the Helpmann Awards. Ursula has also received award nominations for her roles in *Jerry Springer: The Opera* (Sydney Opera House), *Mother Courage and her Children* (Queensland Theatre), *The Wizard of Oz* (Windmill Theatre), *Waltzing the Wilarra* (Yirra Yaakin) and *Magpie Blues*. *Magpie Blues* premiered at the International Cabaret Festival in Adelaide in 2009, playing to packed houses at Darwin Festival, The Dreaming Festival, the Brisbane Cabaret Festival, the Garma Festival in Arnhem Land and as part of the 2010 Melbourne International Arts Festival. Ursula made her directorial debut with *A Letter for Molly* at the Ensemble Theatre in 2022. Her most recent theatre work *Tracker*, co-written with Amy Sole, debuted to full houses at Sydney Festival in 2023. This role is generously supported by Rosemary Hannah & Lynette Preston.

CRIS BALDWIN
SET & COSTUME DESIGNER

Cris is a set & costume designer for theatre, film, live performance and events, also specialising in design development and fabrication for contemporary artists, public artworks and large-scale commercial installations. Designs for theatre include: as set & costume designer: for Belvoir: *Blue*; for Belvoir 25A: *Horses*; for Civic Theatre: *Pirates Code*; for NIDA: *Ah Tuzanbach: Melancholy Cabaret*, *Ex Machina*, *God's Country*, *In a Year With 13 Moons*; as costume designer: for Metro Arts: *The Bluebird Mechanicals*; as associate designer: for Griffin: *Sex Magick*; for 5 Eliza/New Theatricals: *Darkness*; for Belvoir: *Boomkak Panto*; for Red Line Productions at the Old Fitz: *The Seven Deadly Sins & Mahogany Songspiel*; as costume supervisor: for Cross Roads Live: *The Mousetrap* (Australian tour); as costume and props supervisor: for Belvoir/Queensland Theatre: *Fangirls*; as props master: for Belvoir: *Counting and Cracking*; as construction manager/props supervisor: for Belvoir: *Things I Know to be True*, *The Wolves*; as costume/props assistant: for Belvoir: *Dance of Death*; and as costume assistant: for Carriageworks: *Dumy Moyi*. For screen, Cris was Tess Schofield's assistant costume designer for the feature films *The Drover's Wife: The Legend of Molly Johnson* (Bunya/Oombarra Productions) and *Thirteen Lives* (Metro-Goldwyn-Mayer). He was a set designer and 3D modeller on *Thor: Love and Thunder* and a speciality costume maker on *Shang-Chi & The Legend of the Ten Rings* (Marvel Studios). Cris was production & costume designer on Bella Taylor Smith's music video for *Unaware* (Sony EMI), costume designer on Zela Margossian Quintet's music video *The Road*, and production & costume designer on the short film *Last Night* for Prototype. Cris' costumes have been received internationally; in Moscow, his costume *Celcius* was exhibited at the Innovative Costumes of the 21st Century: The Next Generation at the State Historical Museum. He was also finalist in the World of Wearable Art in Wellington, New Zealand. He has also designed events nationally for the Campari Group (Biennale of Sydney 2020–2024, Sydney Contemporary 2021) and tourable sets for live music act Hermitude (International Tour & Aria Awards). A Design graduate of the National Institute of Dramatic Arts, Cris also holds an Advanced Diploma in Fashion Design. In 2023, he was nominated for four Australian Production Design Guild Awards across multiple categories.

VERITY HAMPSON
LIGHTING DESIGNER

Verity's lighting designs for theatre include: for Griffin: *A Strategic Plan*, *And No More Shall We Part*, *Angela's Kitchen*, *Beached*, *Dealing With Clair*, *Dogged*, *Ghosting the Party*, *Jailbaby*, *Orange Thrower*, *Pony*, *The Bleeding Tree*, *The Boys*, *The Bull*, *The Moon and the Coronet of Stars*, *The Floating World*, *Superheroes*, *This Year's Ashes*, *The Turquoise Elephant*; for Griffin Independent: *The Brothers Size*, *The Cold Child*, *Crestfall*, *Family Stories: Belgrade*, *Live Acts On Stage*, *Music*, *The New Electric Ballroom*, *References to Salvador Dali Make Me Hot*, *Way to Heaven*; for Griffin/Bell Shakespeare: *The Literati*; for Bell Shakespeare: *A Midsummer Night's Dream*, *Julius Caesar*, *Titus Andronicus*; for Belvoir: *An Enemy of the People*, *The Blind Giant is Dancing*, *The Drover's Wife*, *Faith Healer*, *Ivanov*, *Sami in Paradise*, *Winyanboga Yurringa*; for Black Swan/Sydney Theatre Company: *City of Gold*; for CAAP/Sydney Festival: *Double Delicious*; for Dancenorth: *Dungarri Nya Nya*; for Ensemble Theatre: *A Doll's House*, *Baby Doll*, *Fully Committed*, *The One*; for Hayes Theatre Co: *Lizzie*; for Malthouse Theatre: *Wake in Fright*; for Queensland Theatre: *Death of a Salesman*; and for Sydney Theatre Company: *7 Stages of Grieving*, *A Raisin in the Sun*, *Blackie Blackie Brown*, *Fences*, *Grand Horizons*, *Hamlet: Prince of Skidmark*, *Home, I'm Darling*, *Machinal*, *Little Mercy*. Verity is a recipient of the Mike Walsh Fellowship and has won three Sydney Theatre Awards, a Green Room Award and an APDG Award for Best Lighting Design.

JESSICA DUNN
COMPOSER & SOUND DESIGNER

Jessica is a composer, sound designer, and performing musician who studied Music at the Sydney Conservatorium of Music. Recent theatre credits include: as composer and sound designer: for Griffin: *A is for Apple*, *Is There Something Wrong With That Lady?*; for Ensemble Theatre: *Photograph 51*; for KXT: *Girl in a School Uniform Walks Into a Bar*; for Legs on the Wall: *Trestle*; for Siren Theatre Co./Seymour Centre: *CAMP*; for State Theatre of South Australia/Sydney Theatre Company: *Chalkface*; for 10 Days on the Island/Tasmanian Theatre Company: *The Mares*; as sound designer: for Sydney Theatre Company: *On the Beach*; as composer: for Legs on the Wall: *Beetle*; as sound programmer: for Sydney Theatre Company: *Julius Caesar*, *The Tempest*; as associate sound designer: for Belvoir: *Counting and Cracking*, *Random*; for Sydney Theatre Company: *Wonnangatta*; as Composer's Assistant: for Sydney Theatre Company: *Harp in the South Parts I & II*; as Performing Musical Director: for Belvoir: *Barbara and the Camp Dogs* (2017 & 2019 seasons); as bassist: for LWA: *SIX the Musical*. Jessica is also Artistic Director of Sirens Big Band, which was awarded the 2020 APRA Arts Music Award for Best Performance for their work on *Bridge of Dreams*.

SANI TOWNSON
CHOREOGRAPHER

Sani comes from a strong cultural family who are of Samu, Koedal, and Dhoeybaw clans of Saibai Island in the Torres Strait. He studied at NAISDA from 1996–2000 and was asked to join Bangarra Dance Theatre from 2001–2006. Since leaving Bangarra, he has been able to work in film and television for SBS, NITV and ABC and has collaborated with companies such as Gondwana Voices, Sydney Children's Choir, QANTAS, Leigh Warren & Dancers, Insite Arts, NAISDA Dance College, Sydney WorldPride and choreographed for artists such as Christine Anu, Felix Riebel, Kate Miller-Heidke, Sean Choolburra and Electric Fields. 2020 saw Sani back in the Bangarra family as the Youth Programs Coordinator while developing and creating his own interactive children's show *Lagaw Mabaygal (Ailan Ppl)*. Earlier this year, Sani created a 15 minute work for Bangarra's DanceClan program, *Kulka*, which explores his Torres Strait Islander bloodline and heritage.

ISABELLA KERDIJK
STAGE MANAGER

Isabella graduated from the production course at the National Institute of Dramatic Art in 2008. She has worked as a stage manager and assistant stage manager on many shows, including: for Griffin: *And No More Shall We Part*, *Green Park*, *Replay*, *Sex Magick*, *The Smallest Hour*, *This Year's Ashes*, *Ugly Mugs*, *Whitefella Yella Tree*, *Wicked Sisters*; for Belvoir: *An Enemy of the People*, *The Dog/The Cat*, *The Drover's Wife*, *Every Brilliant Thing*, *Fangirls*, *Girl Asleep*, *The Glass Menagerie*, *HIR*, *Jasper Jones*, *Kill the Messenger*, *Mother*, *Mother Courage and Her Children*, *My Name is Jimi*, *Stories I Want to Tell You In Person* (National Tour), *The Sugar House*, *Thyestes* (European Tours), *Winyanboga Yurringa*; for Circus Oz: *Cranked Up*; for Darlinghurst Theatre Company: *Fourplay*, *Ride*, *Silent Night*; for Ensemble Theatre: *Benefactors*, *Boxing Day BBQ*, *Rainman*, *The Ruby Sunrise*; for Legs on the Wall: *Bubble*; for LWAA: *The Mousetrap* (Australia/New Zealand Tours); for Spiegelworld: *Empire*; and for Sydney Theatre Company; *Blithe Spirit*. Isabella has worked as production coordinator on *Carmen* (Opera Australia on Sydney Harbour) and production manager/stage manager for *Puppetry of the Penis* (A-List Entertainment). She has also worked on various festivals, including The Garden of Unearthly Delights, Sydney Festival and the Woodford Folk Festival.

TRUE LOVE INTEREST
MATHEW COOPER

Mathew (from Wangatha country) most recently starred in *Hubris & Humiliation* for Sydney Theatre Company. Other theatre credits include: for Griffin: *City of Gold*, *Whitefella Yella Tree* (cover); for Belvoir/ILBIJERRI Theatre Company: *Coranderrk*; for Melbourne Theatre Company/Neon Festival: *Lucky*; for National Theatre of Parramatta: *Stolen*; for Performing Lines: *The Season*; for Queensland Theatre: *Boy Swallows Universe*; for Sydney Theatre Company: *City of Gold*, *Top Coat*; for Yirra Yaakin: *Confessions of a Pyromaniac*, *Cracked*, *The Sum of Us*. On screen, Mathew has been seen in the feature film *The Marshes* and the short film *Last Drinks at Frida's*; and on television in ABC's *Janet King* and *Redfern Now*. He graduated from WAAPA in 2012.

CHANDON
JONATHAN JEFFREY

Jonathan Michael Jeffrey is a proud First Nations man from Darwin, NT. A naturally talented writer, dancer and mentor, Jonathan's personality is characterised by his ability to care and encourage others. He is highly passionate about chasing your dreams and spreading positive messages to inspire others to feel good about themselves. He has very fond memories of performing from a young age that solidified his passion for entertaining. In his early 20s he left Darwin to pursue his greatest desire – a career in the performing arts. Jonathan graduated from the Aboriginal Centre for the Performing Arts in Brisbane and over his years he has performed across the nation. Now based in Sydney, Jonathan is working for Ambience Entertainment as an Associate Producer in Television. He has worked on TV shows such as *Barrumbi Kids* for NITV, *The Garden Hustle* for Channel 9, *Muster Dogs* S2 and *Preppers* for ABC. Most recently Jonathan has starred in Channel 7's *Million Dollar Island* hosted by Ant Middleton.

KYLE
MATTY MILLS

After graduating from WAAPA (Western Australia Academy of Performing Arts) in 2013, proud Kamilaroi man, media personality and actor Matty Mills created waves by covering the Star Observer with a bold statement: "Gay, Black and Proud". He cemented his role in the entertainment industry as a presenter, working for Channel Nine, SBS and NITV. The Deadly Award winner has hosted major national events including the Mardi Gras Online Live Stream, The Dreamtime Awards and the ARIA Awards red carpet coverage. Currently an entertainment reporter for NITV as well as reading the NITV evening news, Matty launched his own IGTV series, *In The Moment with Matty Mills*, showcasing the careers of Indigenous artists and entertainers from around the world. Matty was the the first Indigenous presenter on Nine Network's *Getaway*. His stage premiere was at Sydney Theatre Company with *Top Coat* in 2022.

MOLLY
ANGELINE PENRITH

Angeline is a Wiradjuri and Yuin woman who grew up in the Redfern/Waterloo community. Making her acting debut at 12 years of age by opening for the ABC's *Blackout*, Angeline has gone on to perform in countless film and theatre productions from development to performance. Theatre credits include: for Belvoir: *Wayside Bride/Light Shining in Buckinghamshire*; for Belvoir/Moogahlin Performing Arts: *Winyanboga Yurringa*; for Canute Productions: *Boori Pryor's My Girradundji*; for Sydney Theatre Company: *The Dreaming: Wake Up Australia*. Her television credits include the ABC's *Black Comedy* and *Cleverman*. Angeline has also been involved in numerous play readings and workshops for Griffin, Belvoir, Yellamundie First People's Playwriting Festival and Sydney Theatre Company. She has worked alongside talented directors such as Chris Canute, Leah Purcell and Andrea James. As a community advocate, Angeline believes in self-determination and revival of culture which she has demonstrated in her MC work for NAIDOC at the 2018 Flag Raising Ceremony at NCIE, as well as Yabun Festival.

GINNY/SARAH JANE
STEPHANIE SOMERVILLE

Stephanie is a proud Martu woman. A graduate of the Aboriginal Theatre course and the Acting BA at WAAPA, in her final year she was awarded the Sally Burton Award for Best Female Performance of a Shakespearean Text. Her stage productions include: for Bell Shakespeare: *Macbeth*; for Belvoir 25A: *Slaughterhouse*; for Black Swan State Theatre Company: *The Bleeding Tree*; for The Blue Room Theatre: *MinusOneSister*, *Quokkapocalypse*; for Subiaco Arts Centre: *Lysistrata*; for KXT: *A Little Piece of Ash*; and for Sydney Theatre Company: *Blithe Spirit*, *Chalkface*, *Julius Caesar*. Stephanie was nominated for Best Newcomer at the Sydney Theatre Awards in 2020.

ABOUT GRIFFIN

Griffin is the only theatre company in the country exclusively devoted to the development and staging of new Australian writing. Located in the historic SBW Stables Theatre, nestled in the heart of Kings Cross, Griffin has been Australia's home for the exploration of new stories since 1979.

We are the launch pad for new plays, ideas and writing that other theatres won't take a risk on. We boldly contribute to Australia's unique and powerful storytelling culture. Plays like *Prima Facie*, *Holding the Man* and *City of Gold* all had their world premieres at Griffin before going out to capture the national imagination. In the words of our longest-serving Artistic Director, Ros Horin:

"We are the theatre of first chances."

We are passionate about nurturing emerging and established practitioners alike. We pride ourselves on supporting our vast community of artists, audiences and supporters who consider our theatre their creative home. We help ambitious, bold, risk-taking and urgent Australian work get from the page onto the stage. We tell the stories that help us know who we are as a nation, and who we want to become.

Acknowledgement of Country

Griffin Theatre Company and the SBW Stables Theatre operate and tell stories on the unceded lands of the Gadigal of the Eora Nation. We acknowledge and honour Aboriginal and Torres Strait Islander people as the oldest continuous living culture on the planet, with more than 60,000 years of storytelling practice shaping and underpinning all aspects of Australian culture. It is a privilege that we do not take lightly: to work on this land, and to tell stories on its soil.

GRIFFIN THEATRE COMPANY
13 Craigend St
Gadigal Land
Kings Cross NSW 2011

02 9332 1052
info@griffintheatre.com.au
griffintheatre.com.au

SBW STABLES THEATRE
10 Nimrod St
Gadigal Land
Kings Cross NSW 2011

BOOKINGS
griffintheatre.com.au
02 9361 3817

GRIFFIN FAMILY

Board
Bruce Meagher (Chair)
Guillaume Babille
Nigel Barrington
Simon Burke AO
Julieanne Campbell
Jane Clifford
Lyndell Droga
Declan Greene
Nakul Legha
Julia Pincus
Lenore Robertson
Simone Whetton

Artistic Director & CEO
Declan Greene

Executive Director & CEO
Julieanne Campbell

General Manager
Khym Scott

Associate Artistic Director
Andrea James

Literary Manager
Dylan Van Den Berg

Literary Associate
Julian Larnach

Ticketing Manager
Gary Barker

Ticketing Administrator
Nathan Harrison

Production Manager
Tyler Fitzpatrick

Technical Manager
Sam Gray

Front of House Manager
Alex Bryant-Smith

Front of House
Riordan Berry,
Kandice Joy, Max Philips,
Maddy Withington,
Willo Young

Head of Development
Jake Shavikin

Relationships Manager
Ell Katte

Finance Manager
Kylie Richards

Finance Consultant
Emma Murphy

Marketing Manager
Erica Penollar

Content Producer
Ang Collins

Senior Producer
Leila Enright

Associate Producer
Cassie Hamilton

Administration & Ticketing Coordinator
Kate Marks

Strategic Insights Consultant
Peter O'Connell

Sustainability Coordinators
Ang Collins, Julian Larnach

Brand & Graphic Design
Alphabet

Web Developer
DevQuoll

Cover Photography
Brett Boardman

GRIFFIN DONORS

Income from Griffin activities covers less than 40% of our operating costs—leaving an ever-increasing gap for us to fill through government funding, sponsorship and the generosity of our individual supporters. Your support helps us bridge the gap and keep ticket prices affordable and our work at its best. To make a donation and a difference, contact Griffin on **9332 1052** or donate online at **griffintheatre.com.au**

PROGRAM PATRONS

Griffin Ambassadors
Robertson Foundation

Griffin Amplify
Girgensohn Foundation

Griffin Literary Manager
Robertson Foundation

Griffin Studio
Gil Appleton
Darin Cooper Foundation
Kiong Lee & Richard Funston
Malcolm Robertson Foundation
Geoff & Wendy Simpson OAM
Danielle Smith & Sean Carmody

Griffin Studio Workshop
Mary Ann Rolfe (Patron)
Iolanda Capodanno & Juergen Krufczyk
Darin Cooper Foundation
Bob & Chris Ernst
Susan MacKinnon
Dianne & Peter O'Connell
Merilyn Sleigh & Raoul de Ferranti
Walking up the Hill Foundation

Griffin Women's Initiative
Anonymous (1)
Katrina Barter
Jessica Block
Skye Bouvier
Julieanne Campbell
Iolanda Capodanno
Jane Clifford
Jennifer Darin
Lyndell Droga
Mandy Foley
Judith Fox & Yvonne Stewart
Melinda Graham
Sherry Gregory
Rosemary Hannah & Lynette Preston
Antonia Haralambis
Alexa Haslingden
Page Henty
Ann Johnson
Roanne Knox
Tessa Leong
Tory Loudon
Susan MacKinnon
Sophie McCarthy
Suzie Miller
Sam Mostyn
Julia Pincus
Ruth Ritchie
Lenore Robertson
Deanne Weir
Simone Whetton
Ali Yeldham

PRODUCTION PARTNERS 2023

Jailbaby **by Suzie Miller**
Lisa Barker & Don Russell
Darin Cooper Foundation
Robert Dick & Erin Shiel
Rachel Doyle
Danny Gilbert AM & Kathleen Gilbert
Rosemary Hannah & Lynette Preston
Richard McHugh & Kate Morgan
Bruce Meagher & Greg Waters
Julia Pincus & Ian Learmonth
Andrew Post & Sue Quill
Penelope Wass

SEASON DONORS

Company Patron
$100,000+
Neilson Foundation

Season Patron
$50,000+
Girgensohn Foundation
Robertson Foundation

Mainstage Donors
$20,000+
Anonymous (1)
Darin Cooper Foundation
Robert Dick & Erin Shiel
Rosemary Hannah & Lynette Preston
Julia Pincus & Ian Learmonth
Mary Ann Rolfe

Production Donors
$10,000+
Rachel Doyle
Gordon & Marie Esden
Abraham & Helen James
Ingrid Kaiser
Nathan Mayfield
Richard McHugh & Kate Morgan
Bruce Meagher & Greg Waters
Tim & Sarah Minchin
Dianne & Peter O'Connell
Andrew Post & Susan Quill
Penelope Wass
The WeirAnderson Foundation

Rehearsal Donors
$5,000–$9,999
Anonymous (1)
Gil Appleton
Lisa Barker & Don Russell
Wendy Blacklock
Ellen Borda
Bernard Coles
Ian Dickson
Lyndell & Daniel Droga
Danny Gilbert AM & Kathleen Gilbert
Libby Higgin & Gae Anderson
Ken & Lilian Horler
Lambert Bridge Foundation
Kiong Lee & Richard Funston
Lee Lewis & Brett Boardman
Catriona Morgan-Hunn
Anthony Paull
Rebel Penfold-Russell OAM
Geoff & Wendy Simpson OAM
The Sky Foundation

Merilyn Sleigh & Raoul de Ferranti
Danielle Smith & Sean Carmody
Walking Up the Hill Foundation

Final Draft Donors
$3,000–$4,999
Melissa Ball
Corinne & Bryan
Bob & Chris Ernst
Jocelyn Goyen
Sherry Gregory
James Hartwright & Kerrin D'Arcy
Roanne & John Knox
Susan MacKinnon
Don & Leslie Parsonage
Elizabeth Wing

Workshop Donors
$1,000–$2,999
Anonymous (5)
Antoinette Albert
Baly Douglass Foundation
Katrina Barter
Helen Bauer & Helen Lynch AM
Cherry & Peter Best
Jessica Block
Christy Boyce & Madeleine Beaumont
Dr Bernadette Brennan
Anne Britton
Stephen & Annabelle Burley
Iolanda Capodano & Juergen Krufczyk
Julieanne Campbell
Susie Carleton
Louise Christie
Anna Cleary
Jane Clifford
Bryony & Tim Cox
Sally Crawford
Laura Crennan
Cris Croker & David West
Ros & Paul Espie
Brian Everingham
Jan Ewert
John & Libby Fairfax
Mandy Foley
Sandra Forbes
Hon Ben Franklin MLC
Robert Furley
Jennifer Giles
Global Creatures
Nicky Gluyas

Melinda Graham
Peter Gray & Helen Thwaites
Mink Greene
Kate Halliday
Antonia Haralambis
Kate Harrison
John Head
Mark Hopkinson & Michelle Opie
Michael Jackson
Ann Johnson
David & Adrienne Kitching
Elizabeth Laverty
Benjamin Law
Tessa Leong
Richard & Elizabeth Longes
Tory Loudon
Patricia Lynch
Kyrsty Macdonald & Christopher Hazell
Prudence Manrique
Chris Marrable & Kate Richardson
Sam Mostyn
Lorin Muhlmann
Ian Neuss & Penny Young
David Nguyen
Shaan Perera
Ian Phipps
Martin Portus
Steve Rietoff
Annabel Ritchie
In memory of Katherine Robertson
Sylvia Rosenblum
Jake Shavikin
Jann Skinner
Ann & Quinn Sloan
Geoffrey Starr
Leslie Stern
Stuart Thomas
Elizabeth Thompson
Mike Thompson
Sue Thomson
Janet Wahlquist
Richard Weinstein & Richard Benedict
Simone Whetton
Rob White & Lisa Hamilton
Rosemary White
Paul & Jennifer Winch
Ali Yeldham

Reading Donors
$500–$999
Anonymous (5)
Nicole Abadee & Rob Macfarlan
Brian Abel
Priscilla Adey
Jane Albert
Amity Alexander
Wendy Ashton
Robyn Ayres
Phillip Black
Claire Bornhoffen
Larry Boyd & Barbara Caine AM
Tim Capelin
Jane Christensen
Amanda Clark
David Davie
Michael Diamond & Georgina F
Max Dingle OAM
Elizabeth Diprose
David Earp
Leonie Flannery
Alan Froude & David Round
Peter Graves
Erica Gray
Stephanie & Andrew Harrison
David Hoskins & Paul McKnight
Nicki Jam
Mira Joksovic
Matt Jones & Rebecca Bourne Jones
Colleen Mary Kane
Susan J Kath
Greg Lamont & Gerard Wilmann
Rosemary Lucas & Robert Yuen
Ian & Elizabeth MacDonald
Suzanne & Anthony Maple-Brown
Robert Marks
Nick Read
Simon Marrable & Anna Kasper
Christopher Matthies
Christopher McCabe
John McCallum & Jenny Nicholls
Daniela McMurdo
Dr Stephen McNamara
Jacqui Mercer
John Mitchell
Neville Mitchell
Keith Moynihan
Patricia Novikoff
Carolyn Penfold
Belinda Piggott & David Ojerholm
Virginia Pursell
A.O. Redmond
Bill Harris

Gemma Rygate
Rob & Rae Spence
Mary Stollery & Eric Dole
Catherine Sullivan & Alexandra Bowen
Ariadne Vromen
Robyn Fortescue & Rosie Wagstaff
David & Jennifer Watson
Julie Whitfield
Helen Wicker

**First Draft Donors
$200-$499**
Anonymous (9)
Susan Ambler
Elizabeth Antonievich
William Armitage
Chris Baker
Jan Barr
John Bell AO, OBE
Edwina Birch
Peter Brown
Wendy Buswell
Ruth Campbell
David Caulfield
Sue Clark
Amanda Connelly
Edward Cooper & Daniel Zucker
Louise Costanzo
Bryan Cutler
Sue Donnelly
Peter Duerden
Anna Duggan
Kathy Esson
Elizabeth Evatt
Michael Eyers
Helen Ford
Eva Gerber
Jock Given
Deane Golding
Keith Gow
Virginia & Kieran Greene
Jo Grisard
Edwina Guinness
Ruth Guss
Kate Haddock
Jan Harland
Raewyn Harlock
Robert Henderson & Marijke Conrade
Grania Hickley
Sylvia Hrovatin
Matthew Huxtable
Marian & Nabeel Ibrahim
Andrew Inglis
James Landon-Smith
Penelope Latey
Liz Locke
Anna Logan
Danielle Long
Norman Long
Noella Lopez
George & Maruschka Loupis
Anni MacDougall
Claire McCaughan
Louise McDonald
Duncan McKay
Paula McLean
Anne Miehs
Julia Mitchell
Mark Mitchell
Sarah Mort
Margaret Murphy
Carolyn Newman
Suzanne Osmond
Catherine & Joshua Sylvia HrovatinPalmer
Peter Pezzutti
Christopher Powell
Janelle Prescott
Andrew Pringle
Dorothy & Adit Rao
Tracey Robson
Ann Rocca
Michael & Noelleen Rosen
Catherine Rothery
Kevin & Shirley Ryan
Dimity Scales
Julia Selby
Vivienne Skinner
Bridget Smith
Vanda & Martin Smith
James, Beu & Sue
Augusta Supple
Margaret Teh
Danny Tomic
Rachel Trigg
Samantha Turley
Adam Van Rooijen
Eve Wynhausen
William Zappa

We would also like to thank Peter O'Connell for his expertise, guidance and time.

CURRENT AS OF 15 JULY 2023

GRIFFIN SPONSORS

Griffin would like to thank the following:

OUR PARTNERS

Government Supporters   Benefactor

Creative Partners

Company Sponsors

Griffin Theatre Company is assisted by the Australian Government through the Australia Council, its arts funding and advisory body; and the NSW Government through Create NSW.

www.ingramcontent.com/pod-product-compliance
Lightning Source LLC
Chambersburg PA
CBHW050022090426
42734CB00021B/3374